Rhythm & Chops Builders

Timing and Technique Exercises for the Modern Drummer

by Bill Bachman

Edited by Willie Rose and Michael Dawson

Interior design and layout by Scott Bienstock

Cover design by Richard Leeds

Cover photo by Spencer Moon
Back cover photo by Mat Duniam
Interior photos by Mat Duniam, Cera Jaso, and Leslie Li

Published by:
Modern Drummer Publications, Inc.
271 Route 46 West
Suite H-212
Fairfield, NJ 07004 USA

Contents

Acknowledgements

Thanks to my family, Vita, Sophia, Lydia, and Daniel, for making every day an adventure, to Mike Dawson at *Modern Drummer* for his fantastic editing prowess and support in making this second book, to the readers of *Modern Drummer* for their enthusiasm and kind words for my content in the Strictly Technique column, to my former teachers and current teachers (aka students), to Vic Firth sticks, Remo drumheads, and Zildjian cymbals for their support, and to the Lord who created us in His image with a sense of rhythm and creative thought!

Introduction

Welcome to *Rhythm & Chops Builders*! The goal of this book is to help develop, expand, and solidify your rhythmic vocabulary, accuracy, and comfort level, and to build chops on top of that. Although this book opens with a brief section discussing hand technique, it's best used in conjunction with my other book, *Stick Technique*, which focuses on your technical approach to build loose, flowing, powerful, and fast hands that are well-trained in motion and vocabulary. The two books are complementary, not sequential.

The Rhythm Builders in this method are meant to build your rhythmic vocabulary and make you much more comfortable, confident, and accurate. The rhythms will go from common to obscure, and there are certainly some challenges. As you train your mind, body, and musical instinct with new and familiar rhythms through thousands of repetitions, they'll confidently and effortlessly come out in creative ways in the music that you play.

The Chops Builders are an expansion of the exercises found in *Stick Technique*, although many of the exercises in this book borrow from the rhythmic concepts covered in this method's Rhythm Builders section. Ultimately, all of the Chops Builders in both books are just collections of great things to work on to develop your hands, mind, vocabulary, and chops, and there's no particular sequence to them.

Technique

INTRODUCTION

The following section covers techniques that are used throughout *Rhythm and Chops Builders* (refer to my book *Stick Technique* for a more comprehensive technical overview). We'll dive into the following stroke techniques:

Free stroke (aka full stroke or legato stroke). This loose, rebounding stroke is the foundation of efficient drumming technique. It's used when playing successive strokes at the same stick height and dynamic level.

Alley-oop. This is a wrist/finger combination technique that's used when playing diddles (double strokes) and triple strokes. This technique is necessary at tempos where the wrists can't play multiple-note combinations without tensing up.

Downstroke, tap, and upstroke. Downstrokes and upstrokes are just like free strokes, except that after you hit the drum, the stick heights are modified in order to play subsequent strokes at a lower dynamic level. Taps are low free strokes.

Moeller whip stroke. This technique involves playing downstrokes and upstrokes from the forearm when the wrist would otherwise get overworked and stiffen up. The Moeller whip stroke is crucial for playing accent patterns with a smooth and effortless flow, especially at fast tempos.

So, how do you choose when to use a certain technique? The technique you use will be determined by the type of rudiment or pattern being played, the instrument being played, the dynamic level, and the tempo. Once the various techniques are mastered, your hands will automatically choose the one that allows you to perform in the most effective and efficient way possible.

The bottom line is that in order to develop a wide vocabulary on the drums, you need to have a lot of techniques at your disposal. Building technique requires thousands of correct repetitions ("perfect practice") in order to train your muscle memory. While there are no shortcuts to developing good technique, the material in this book is designed to help you get there as quickly as possible.

FREE STROKE

The free stroke, which is also commonly referred to as the full stroke or the legato stroke, is the most important technique you should learn, as it's the foundation for almost every other stroke type. The free stroke is basically a dribble of the stick where you throw the stick down toward the drum and then let it rebound off the drumhead so that it returns to the height where it started. Free strokes should be used for everything played at one stick height where there's no logical reason to hold the stick down near the drumhead. Free strokes require a solid fulcrum and very relaxed hands.

Some drummers even feel as if they're cheating when they first learn to execute this stroke.

A properly played free stroke proves two things about your technique. First, it shows that the stroke was played with enough velocity into the drum so that it could rebound back up to the starting point. Second, it shows that the hand is relaxed enough that the stick could rebound without being disrupted by tension. Practicing free strokes is a great way to loosen up your hands and improve your consistency and sound quality.

The more you hold on to the stick and manipulate its motion, the greater the chance for human error and inconsistency, and the more stress you put on your hands. Conversely, if you relax and let physics carry the workload, your playing will have increased flow and consistency, and you'll put less stress on the hands.

Volume is determined more by how *fast* you move the stick to hit the drum rather than by how hard you strike. To get the most sound out of your instrument, focus on playing big and loose free strokes with high velocity, instead of simply hitting hard with a lot of inertia through the drumhead. You'll not only produce more volume with less effort, but you'll also have a more natural/musical sound, and will be able to play faster and with more endurance. Plus you'll do less damage to your hands and to your equipment.

Free-Stroke Technique

To play a free stroke, start with the sticks held in the "up" position, with the wrists turned up and the fingers held partially open.

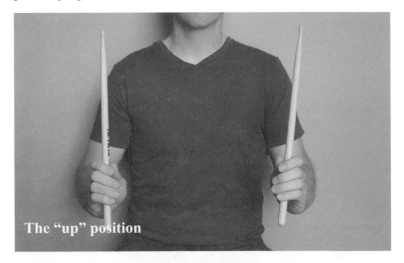

The "up" position

Throw the stick down toward the drum using the wrist and all four fingers to accelerate it. With the hand held loose, let the stick hit the drum with all of its velocity and freely rebound back up to where it started. The key is to quickly accelerate the stick and then immediately relax the hand. It's helpful to think about playing big strokes where you throw the stick down fast—but not hard.

When playing free strokes, the butt end of the stick should

never hit the palm of your hand, or else some of the stick's energy will be absorbed into the hand and won't make it to the drum. If the fingers hold the stick against the palm, there will be extra tension in the hand, which results in less acceleration and a stiffer sound. When everything is working properly, the stick should feel heavy and should resonate fully with a high-pitched sound.

It's very important to locate the fulcrum on the stick at the point where it rebounds most freely. If you choke up too far, the stick doesn't rebound very well. Likewise, if you hold the stick too far back, the stick doesn't rebound well and you also get an uncomfortable vibration from the stick into the back fingers. The fulcrum should be located where the stick does the most work for you, and the stick should be held just tightly enough that you don't drop it. In matched grip, be sure to allow the end of the first finger to operate separately from the fulcrum point so that you can use the tip of the finger to play the stick.

Free strokes can be played with various ratios of wrist to finger. Favoring the wrist over the fingers will result in bigger and louder strokes, since the stick moves in a larger arch.

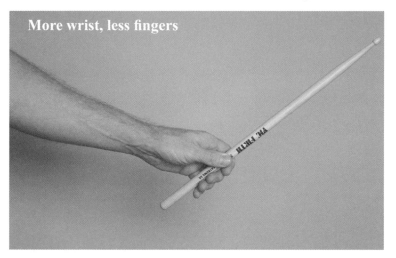

More wrist, less fingers

Favoring finger use, which focuses on the fulcrum between the thumb and first or second finger, results in smaller strokes that can be desirable for greater finesse and speed, especially at lower stick heights and softer volumes.

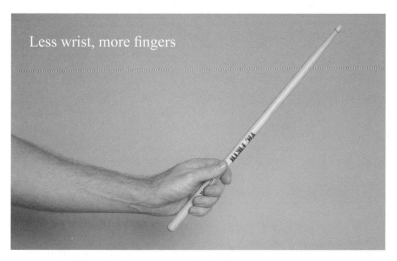

Less wrist, more fingers

It's ideal to have the technical ability to play at either end of the spectrum (finger or wrist strokes) and to have the ability to gradually morph from one to the other.

Developing the Free Stroke

When first learning the free stroke, most drummers feel they're cheating, or they feel somewhat out of control since they're used to doing so much more work. "More work" simply means more tension, and more tension generally slows down your strokes and robs you of sound quality and flow. What initially feels out of control and lazy will become comfortable once you've practiced it long enough to achieve the proper muscle memory.

Begin by practicing individual free strokes that start and stop past vertical. To get past vertical, you must open your fingers a bit. You want your fingers to be in a position to play the stick rather than hold it. Don't rob yourself of the potential speed and flow generated by using the fingers in addition to the wrist to accelerate the stroke. (When playing free strokes with French grip, limit the stick height to as high as the thumb will allow without the fulcrum changing.) Focus more on the stick's return to the "up" position than the hand action used to play the free stroke, since the stick's motion *after* striking the drum tends to be a telltale sign of whether or not the free stroke was played correctly.

Once your individual free strokes are comfortable and consistent, start stringing them together as consecutive dribbles of the stick. After these consecutive free strokes are feeling comfortable and are consistently returning past vertical, practice them at lower stick heights. As the tempo goes up, the stick heights come down.

Be careful not to neglect the wrist once you're comfortable opening the fingers and using them to accelerate the stroke. If you find that your pinkie can't reach the stick, or it barely touches the side of the stick, then you need to raise the wrist higher so that the pinkie can reach the front of the stick. This will result in a healthy balance of wrist and finger use for playing free strokes.

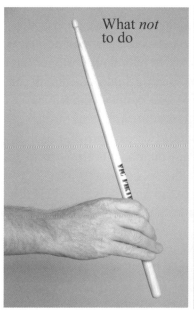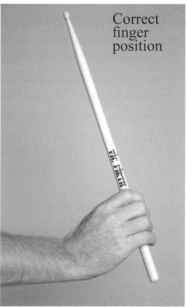

What *not* to do

Correct finger position

I always have students begin by playing free strokes using just the fulcrum and the end of the first finger, while the three back fingers hang completely off the stick. From there we add the fingers one at a time.

This hand position isolates the foundation of the free stroke, which is the fulcrum and the end of the first finger. Once the first finger is playing the stick well, I have students add one finger at a time, making sure that the sound and flow don't change throughout.

ALLEY-OOP

The alley-oop technique is what I call a wrist/finger free-stroke combination used for playing double strokes (diddles) and triple strokes. While it can be likened to the push/pull technique, which is a wrist stroke followed by a finger stroke, the alley-oop isn't intended for playing ongoing, evenly metered strokes. It's a technique for playing short bursts of two or three notes.

The initial stroke, "alley," is played mainly from the wrist and uses a higher stick height with slower acceleration. The second stroke, "oop," is played from the fingers and uses a lower stick height and faster acceleration in order to match the volume of the initial stroke. The alley-oop requires quick finger technique in order to accelerate the second stroke. When playing low doubles, it might be helpful to think of the alley-oop as a drop-catch technique where the hand drops the stick and then the fingers catch it into the palm, adding a bit of velocity to the second stroke. The fingers also have to relax after their strokes so that the stick can bounce up to the starting position. As complicated as this may sound, the alley-oop technique is the best way to play double strokes and triple strokes, and it will start happening automatically as you increase the tempo of your free-stroke doubles and triples.

Many drummers struggle with double and triple strokes. The problems often fall into one of two categories: relying too heavily on bounce or stroking each beat entirely from the wrist. If you simply bounce the second and third strokes, they will sound weaker than the first stroke because they have less velocity going into the drum. If you stroke everything from the wrist, your speed will be limited. Plus you'll lose sound quality, your hands will get tight, and you'll risk wrist injury since you'll be asking the wrists to do too much.

Once you've developed strong finger control, you'll not only be able to play well-balanced doubles and triples, but you'll also be able to crescendo within them to add dynamic contour within roll patterns. It takes time and practice to develop the ability to play the finger strokes with good velocity, but it's worth it.

Alley-Oop Technique

To play alley-oop doubles, play a free stroke at a high stick height, using mainly the wrist, and let the stick rebound back up as much as possible before playing the second stroke.

When playing very slow doubles, both notes are played as identical free strokes, since there's time for the hand and stick to come all the way back up. As you play faster doubles, however, there's not enough time for the hand to come all the way up to play the second stroke. This is where the alley-oop technique becomes necessary.

At faster tempos, the second stroke (which is also a free stroke) will need to be played with more fingers than wrist, from a lower stick height. You'll need to move the stick with greater velocity in order to match the volume of the first stroke, since the first stroke was played at a higher stick height. Remember that volume is determined by the *speed* of the stroke, not the stick height.

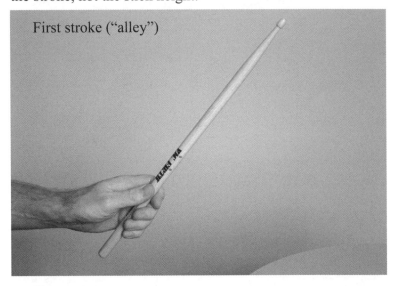
First stroke ("alley")

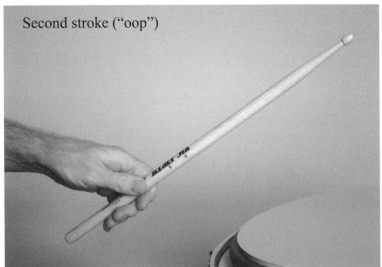
Second stroke ("oop")

To summarize the alley-oop technique, the first note should be played mainly with the wrist and the second stroke should be played mainly with the fingers (though the wrist can move a bit for the second stroke too). As you increase the speed of the double or triple stroke, the stick height will naturally drop with each subsequent stroke. But if you play the rebound strokes with higher velocity than the first (using the fingers), it's possible to get a well-balanced and even sound.

Once the alley-oop technique is working, you should be able to watch the top of your hand throw down the first stroke and then the fingers "slam dunk" the second stroke. Remember that unless you're playing at medium-fast tempos and above, all of the notes are played as free strokes. The stick should resonate freely with a high pitch as it rebounds back up on its own. Keep the hand relaxed.

Alley-Oop Stroke Types: Free/Free Versus Free/Down

Alley-oop doubles can be played as two free strokes or as a free stroke and a downstroke where the stick stops close to the drum. Both methods are viable, but there are times when one or the other is preferable due to physical demands or musical application. At slow and medium-slow tempos, the second stroke should be a free stroke that's played more by the fingers than the wrists. Playing both strokes as free strokes works in this tempo range because there's time for the stick to float back up after the diddle.

At medium-fast tempos and above, the second stroke will need to become a downstroke. In this tempo range, there isn't enough time for the fingers to open and allow the stick to float up after either stroke. Instead, the rebound of the first stroke pushes the fingers open, and then the fingers grab the stick into the palm, which accelerates the stick and adds the necessary velocity so that the volume of the second stroke matches that of the first stroke. This technique also makes the second stroke a downstroke.

You'll get a bigger, smoother, and rounder sound with less effort if you work up the finesse required to play doubles as free/free strokes at applicable tempos. Unless they're desired for musical effect or they're required because you're playing on a mushy playing surface (like a floor tom), try to avoid playing doubles as a free stroke/ downstroke combination, because the second notes can sound forced, stiff, and choked.

Fast Alley-Oop Doubles

When playing faster double-stroke rolls (roughly 32nd notes at 90 bpm and up), the alley-oop technique must be modified in order to prevent wrist strain. At this point, the forearms will be added to provide relief. When the rolls get very fast (roughly 32nd notes at 130 bpm and up), the wrists aren't really used much at all, and the alley-oop becomes forearm and fingers rather than wrist and fingers.

It's helpful to play fast rolls with an "on top of the stick" posture, where the wrists point downward slightly, relative to the forearm, and the sticks point down toward the drum at a steeper angle. This posture gives you more leverage to push into the drum as your forearms pump to play the first note and the front two fingers accelerate the second. (At very high speeds, it's unrealistic for the back two fingers to move far and quickly enough to maintain contact with the stick.)

Triple Strokes: Alley-Oop-Oop

When applying the alley-oop technique to triple strokes, simply add a third stroke played mainly from the fingers. The first note should be made mostly with the wrist, and the second and third strokes should be made mainly with the fingers (though the wrist does move a bit). The stick will naturally drop down with each stroke, but if you play the second and third strokes with greater and greater velocity (from the fingers), it's possible to get a well-balanced, even sound.

At slow to medium tempos, your hands should be completely relaxed after throwing down the third stroke so that the stick can rebound on its own. At fast tempos, the free/free/downstroke combination will need to be used. No arm motion is necessary because there's plenty of time for the hand to reset without any strain.

Developing the Alley-Oop Technique

Don't overanalyze and exaggerate the wrist/finger motion in the alley-oop and alley-oop-oop techniques. Practice the motion slowly so that it's more like two or three free strokes played from the wrist. As you gradually increase the speed, the fingers will automatically start to kick in on the second and third strokes.

To develop the all-important finger control required in the alley-oop and alley-oop-oop techniques, practice as many repetitions as possible, making sure that the last stroke in the double or triple is played as a true free stroke and rebounds all the way back up on its own. If you practice faster than a tempo at which you can accomplish this correctly, then you're not developing the correct technique.

Try not to squeeze the stick with the front two fingers to control the bounce, but instead focus on building finger control so that even at fast tempos you can still use at least the front two fingers to punch the rebound strokes with extra velocity.

After focusing on the free/free method for alley-oop doubles, I recommend also building up the free stroke/ downstroke approach where you accent the second beat of the double as a downstroke, with extra velocity from the fingers. I find it preferable to invert the roll (RLLR or LRRL) so that the accented second notes land on the downbeats rather than on the upbeats.

DOWNSTROKES, TAPS, AND UPSTROKES

If we used only free strokes, our playing would become pretty dull, since every note would be played at the same stick height and dynamic level. In order to add accents and dynamic contour to the music, you'll need to modify the free stroke into downstrokes and upstrokes.

The downstroke starts high and stops down close to the head. This stroke is used to transition from an accent to a tap. The upstroke starts low and ends high and is used to transition from a tap to an accent. It's important to understand that the free stroke is the foundation for both downstrokes and upstrokes. The more control of downstrokes and upstrokes you have, the more dynamic your music will become.

Downstrokes

First let's look at the downstroke in matched grip. The downstroke is also commonly referred to as a "staccato" stroke. *Staccato* is the musical term meaning short and seperated, which in this case refers to the accent's hand motion being short and seperated from the following taps. The downstroke is just like the free stroke until a split second after you hit the drum, when the stick should be squeezed against the palm of the hand (the brakes) in order to absorb the stick's energy and stop it low to the drum for a following tap. Squelching the stick's rebound against the brakes will have a little bit of physical impact, and it will cut off some of the stick's resonance. This is okay. Just be sure to avoid staying on the brakes the entire time you play the downstroke. At the top of the stroke, the butt end of the stick should be off the palm so that the stick is loose in the hand and the wrist and fingers have the opportunity to accelerate the stick toward the drum. Keeping the stick against the palm the entire time is like driving with one foot on the gas and one foot on the brake and will result in a tight, stiff, and ultimately slower stroke.

It's helpful to think about the following statement when playing downstrokes: *Downstrokes point down*. This posture gives you some leverage, which is helpful in quickly squelching the stick's rebound. In order for the downstroke to point down, you must play on top of the stick so that the fulcrum is held higher than the bead of the stick. This puts the hand in a position where immediately after gripping the stick against the palm, the wrist can drop down in order for the fingers to open up and freely play the stick. (Playing on top of the stick will also help avoid accidental rimshots when playing downstrokes.)

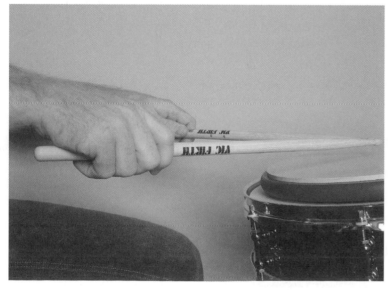

It's crucial that the thumb is located a bit on the top side of the stick (American grip) so that it's in a good position to push down against the stick's natural rebound. The challenge is to develop the ability to hit the brakes quickly and then quickly release the brakes so that your fingers are ready to loosely play the next stroke.

Taps and Upstrokes

Taps are very simple once you've mastered the free stroke, since they're nothing more than low free strokes. When playing taps, avoid squeezing the stick against the brakes, though the stick can lightly touch the palm. The stick should feel heavy, and it should resonate freely.

The upstroke is also very simple. It starts as a tap stroke (or low free stroke), but immediately after you hit the drum you lift up the stick in preparation for an accent. Avoid squeezing the stick against the brakes while playing the stroke and while lifting the stick. You want the fingers to be in an open position at the top of the upstroke so they're prepared to accelerate the stick for the following stroke. Other than when the fingers squeeze the stick during a downstroke, you want the fingers to help play the stick and not squeeze the stick.

Putting It All Together: Full, Down, Up, and Tap Strokes

To play patterns with accents and taps you'll need to use all four basic strokes (full, down, up, and tap). The full stroke is a high stroke that starts and ends high. (Full strokes are the same as free strokes and should be played where the stick is allowed to rebound back up on its own.) The downstroke is a high stroke that ends low. The upstroke is a low stroke that ends high. The tap stroke is a low stroke that stays low. (Tap strokes should be played as low free strokes with relaxed hands and without squeezing the stick against the palm.)

The stroke type you use within a given rhythm or rudiment is determined by the stroke height of the following note played by the same hand. Downstrokes and upstrokes should be used when the following stroke is played at a new stick height. When there is no change in stick height for the following note, the free stroke should be used (at the full- or tap-stroke height). The goal is to play free strokes as often as possible in order to play as loosely as possible. Play downstrokes only when necessary.

Here's another way of looking at it: Every stroke within an accent/tap pattern will be played smoothly and relaxed, and the butt end of the stick will never get squeezed against the brakes, with the exception of the downstrokes. Aside from the times when you need to use downstrokes, every other stroke should remain relaxed and flowing so that the stick feels heavy and resonates freely in a loosely held hand.

Developing Downstrokes, Taps, and Upstrokes

I don't recommend playing downstrokes before mastering the free stroke, since the free stroke is your foundation. If you start playing advanced vocabulary containing various accents and taps before you've mastered the free stroke, you could end up with a tight grip that will take a long time to remedy.

When playing accented passages using this technique, no tap should be louder or softer than any other tap, and no accent should be louder or softer than any other accent. The goal is to develop complete control over very high accents and very low taps so that ultimately you can decide what stick heights you want to use in a given musical situation.

Rhythmic accuracy is also extremely important while you're training yourself to perform these key hand motions. Set your metronome to play the smallest subdivisions you're practicing, and try to bury the metronome, which means you're so locked in that you don't hear the clicks.

With straight-8th-note exercises, I recommend starting at 100 bpm and going up in ten-beat increments.

MOELLER WHIP STROKE AND MOELLER WHIP-STROKE COMBINATION

The Moeller whip stroke is named after Sanford "Gus" Moeller, a famous teacher from the early 1900s who became known for teaching a whipping motion used by Civil War drummers. In recent years, "Moeller" has become a buzzword for good technique, and many have turned it into an elusive mystery.

A Moeller stroke is simply a whip stroke, used for accents, played from the forearm instead of the wrist, but the "Moeller technique" (or "Moeller method") is an approach involving a whipped accent followed by freely rebounding taps. To delineate the two techniques, I'll refer to them as the "Moeller whip stroke" and the "Moeller whip-stroke combination."

When using the Moeller whip stroke, the forearm lifts up the hand, which hangs limp, and then the stick is whipped down in order to achieve the accent. The forearm drags the hand and stick up and down, so the forearm is always the first thing to move and the stick is always the last thing to move. It may be helpful to think about playing the stroke with the palm of the hand (or the end of the forearm) while letting the hand and stick naturally find their way to the drum slightly after the fact.

The Moeller whip downstroke, or what I call the "whip-and-stop," should be used when there's time to stop the stick low after the accent preceding the next low tap. The Moeller whip-stroke combination (whip-and-flop) should be used when there's a tap immediately following the accent and you want to flow into it, or where a smooth and effortless flow is desired over maximum dynamic contrast. Either way, the Moeller whip approach should be applied when playing accent/tap rudiments and patterns at high speeds in order to prevent the wrists from tightening up.

Moeller Whip Stroke

To play a full-size Moeller whip stroke in matched grip, hold the sticks in the American or German position so that the butt end pokes out to the side of the hand. (Moeller will also work in French grip, but only with a much smaller motion due to the wrist's limited side-to-side range of motion.)

You may also want to use the second-finger fulcrum instead of the first-finger fulcrum, since more of the energy of the whip will transfer to the stick when you hold it with the second finger, and you won't need intricate finger finesse when applying this technique.

Hold on to the stick with your fulcrum just tight enough that you don't drop the stick. Starting with the sticks near the drum, let the wrist relax as you pick up the entire arm from the shoulder. (It may help to think about the upper arm dragging up the forearm, hand, and stick.) At this point the hand and stick should be dangling and pointing down toward the drum. While keeping the wrist totally relaxed, throw the arm down. In the blink of an eye, the arm passes the hand and stick, and the hand and stick are now pointing up relative to the forearm. At this point, the hand is whipped toward the drum faster than the forearm, and the stick is whipped toward the drum faster than the hand. *Boom!*

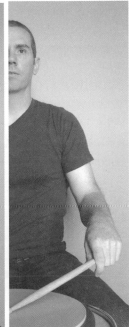

After striking the drum, you can either stop the stick near the head (downstroke) or let it rebound back up by opening the fingers. Either way, it's important that you don't lift the forearm back up immediately after the Moeller whip stroke. The arm should stay down and relax.

As the tempo increases, the size of the Moeller whip-stroke motion will need to decrease.

This is why the Moeller whip stroke is more commonly played from the forearm and not the upper arm. As the speed increases even more, the motion should continue to decrease. At very high speeds, the Moeller whip stroke will look like nothing more than a twitch of the wrist, which is actually the forearm throwing down slightly in order to make the hand and stick rise relative to the forearm. At this point, there's also the effect of the palm bumping down the butt end of the stick in order to pop up the front end.

A pure Moeller whip stroke doesn't engage the wrist muscles. It's impossible for the wrist to throw down at the speed of the whip, so engaging the muscles that control the wrist will just slow down the stroke, add tension, and defeat the whipping motion.

Moeller Upstroke

When a low tap immediately precedes an accent and you want to use the Moeller whip technique, you'll need to play a Moeller upstroke. Think of this as a preparation stroke used to set up the Moeller whip-stroke accent. Here, the stick works like a seesaw. As the back of the stick gets picked up, the front drops down and plays an incidental tap. Don't intentionally play the upstroke by engaging the wrist or fingers. It may be helpful to think of dragging the hand and stick up away from the drum with the forearm as the stroke is played. Also, don't lift the arm prior to playing this tap, because then you would have to engage your wrist muscles in order to play the tap. (This is the most common mistake made when learning Moeller upstrokes.)

The Moeller upstroke should just drop in and hit the drum as a droopy tap. Feel the forearm lift and the wrist drop down (like a dog paw) at the same time as the tap is played incidentally (the seesaw effect). If it feels lazy and out of control, you're probably doing it right. With practice, you'll develop enough finesse to ensure that these incidental taps hit the drum with rhythmic accuracy.

Moeller Whip-Stroke Combination (Whip-and-Flop Technique)

When drummers speak of the Moeller technique or the Moeller method, they're often talking about a system of applying the Moeller whip stroke within groups of accents and taps. The idea is to start with a Moeller whip stroke and then let the stick rebound freely into one or more bounce taps before repeating the cycle. No physical work is involved in playing the taps. The constant motion of this whip-and-flop technique takes stress off the body.

It may help to look at the Moeller whip-stroke combination in this manner: Your forearm drags the hand and stick up and down, while lazy bounce taps drop in between the accents.

The Moeller whip-stroke combination is most often used when playing consecutive sets of two notes (accent, tap), three notes (accent, tap, tap), or four notes (accent, tap, tap, tap) with the same hand. The accents are all played as Moeller whip strokes, and the taps in the middle are bounces. The last tap preceding the next accent is a Moeller upstroke. The goal is to get two or more strokes from one whipping motion. (As you get into groupings of four notes and more, finger control will start to become necessary to keep the taps going, since the accent's energy will gradually dissipate.)

The forearms pick up the stick for the Moeller upstroke only on the very last tap preceding the accent. If you lift the arms prior to that, the rebound potential of the inner taps is reduced, the sound of the taps changes, and the velocity of the upcoming Moeller whip stroke is preemptively slowed down.

With the Moeller whip-stroke combination, you'll need to sacrifice the height accuracy of the low taps in order to maximize flow. The volume contrast between the accents and taps is now determined almost exclusively by the velocity of the strokes. The whip stroke is much faster than the taps and will therefore be louder than the following bounce-stroke taps.

You want to put the smoothness and flow of the Moeller whip-stroke combination ahead of the bigness of the accents. Don't punch the accents too hard, or else you'll have to hit the brakes in order to keep the next tap from coming in too early.

Developing the Moeller Whip Stroke and the Moeller Whip-Stroke Combination

I recommend working on the Moeller method *after* mastering the four basic wrist-stroke techniques (free stroke, downstroke, tap, and upstroke). The wrist strokes are the fundamentals, while the Moeller method falls in the category of "break the rules after you've learned them." While the Moeller method lends itself to a relaxed and flowing behind-the-beat feel, you should also have good wrist-stroke technique, since both approaches have their advantages and disadvantages.

Moeller whip strokes should first be learned as big, full motions starting from the shoulder. This allows you to fully understand the magnitude of the power available with this stroke. The size of the motion should be reduced as the tempo increases.

It's also beneficial to practice the motion without sticks in order to make sure that the hand is held limp and is relaxed. (See the following photos.)

After getting the feel of the motion without sticks, add a stick between your thumb and second finger (or between your thumb and first finger in traditional grip). Use just enough pressure so as not to drop the stick. Continue to practice the motion with and without the stick until your hand feels about the same either way. Remember that any use of the muscles that control the wrist will kill the whip.

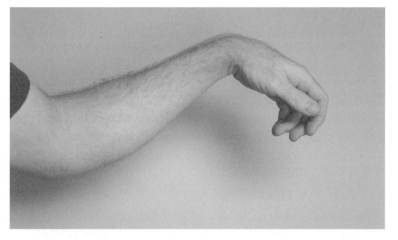

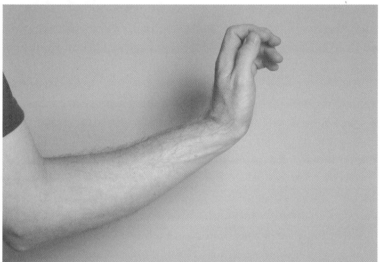

Rhythm Builders

Rhythm and Timing

Part 1: Three-Note 16th Groupings

Over these first five chapters we're going to develop not only timing and rhythmic accuracy with triplets and 16th notes, but also accent/tap control using the four basic strokes (full, down, tap, and up). To some, the exercises will look simple, but playing them perfectly with great dynamic contrast and a smooth, musical feel is deceptively hard, especially at very slow and very fast tempos.

The first exercise in each section will be played with an all-accented check pattern leading into the chosen rhythms (also accented), with all of the subdivisions filled in as taps. This will help guide the accented rhythm to the correct place and will also serve as a great opportunity to examine stick-height accuracy and dynamic contrast. The second exercise in each chapter will contain the same accented rhythms, but the taps will be taken away and you'll play what was the accented rhythm at one stick height and as free strokes.

With all of the exercises, use your metronome and tap your foot. Count all of the played notes out loud at first, and then count just quarter notes. Be sure to get all of the motions correct, as they are designed to flow and make it much easier to play with rhythmic accuracy. Play the exercises with the left hand leading as well, in order to develop balanced hands and confidence leading with the weaker side. It'll take thousands of perfect repetitions to program these rhythms into your musical vocabulary. If you find yourself thinking or doing math in your head, then keep repeating the exercise.

To start, we'll look at the four different three-note 16th groupings. The first will be "1-e-&." Then we'll move the grouping back to "e-&-a." We'll keep moving it back to "1-&-a" and finally "1-e-a." The first exercise, which has the chosen rhythms accented, will be tricky to play, since there are more accents than taps. (It's usually the opposite.) To help, we've labeled the stroke type below each note (F = full, D = down, T = tap, and U = up).

Don't be afraid to practice the patterns extremely slowly in order to train your hands to play the appropriate stroke types. The fastest way to develop coordination is by practicing accurately but very slowly. If the full, tap, and upstrokes aren't played completely relaxed, or if the downstrokes aren't stopped low to the drum, you won't achieve the desired musical effect. Simply put, if your hands don't know what's coming next, then they'll end up fudging through with either too much tension or a lack of accent/tap stick-height clarity.

Once your hands know what's coming, be sure to exaggerate the high and low stick heights for maximum dynamic contrast. And don't pound the downstroke accents. They need to relate dynamically to the flowing stream of accents in the check patterns. The exercise is in a 4-2-1 format where you play four of each variation, then two, then one, and repeat it.

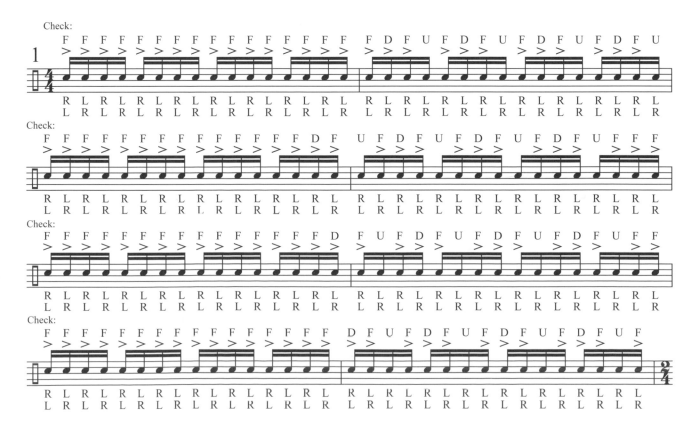

Now it's time to play it all at one stick height with the three-note groupings isolated. The key to rhythmic accuracy will be in the flowing motion of the free strokes. The check pattern should flow into the broken rhythms, and the last of the broken rhythms should flow right back into the check pattern.

With these three-note 16th patterns, one hand will flow smoothly through each check-pattern/broken-rhythm/check-pattern combo. Learn to trust your hands to flow into the rhythms accurately without too much thought. It's crucial to play the correct strokes so that the patterns flow smoothly into one another. Also be sure to play the space (at least initially) by subdividing the partials in your head, which were played as taps in the first exercise.

I recommend playing this second exercise initially with the free strokes flowing up to the greatest stick height that's comfortable and easily sustainable. Then play it at a piano (soft) dynamic level to work on your finesse.

Here are some free-stroke guidelines to keep in mind.
1. Free strokes start and stop at the same height.
2. Never pick up the stick; only throw it down.
3. The back of the stick will never touch the palm of your hand.
4. Make sure the sticks feel heavy and resonate with a high pitch as you dribble them.

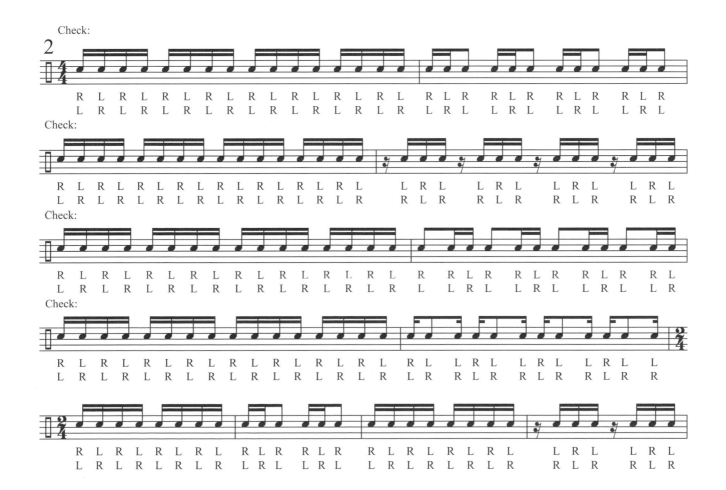

Once you've got these patterns under control, it's time to do them over and over again. It's not that hard to understand them, but training your muscle memory and ingraining an accurate, musical feel takes time and thousands of repetitions.

Rhythm and Timing

Part 2: Two-Note 16th Groupings

Next we're going to focus on the six different two-note 16th-note groupings. We'll begin with "1-e," and then we'll move to "e-&," then "&-a," and finally "1-a." After those first four variations, we'll do a separate exercise for the last two two-note groupings: "1-&" and the ever-tricky "e-a." As in the previous section, the exercises will first focus on playing the rhythms as accents among taps, and then we'll play the rhythms with the spaces between them left open.

The first exercise, with the accents and taps, will most likely be easier to play than the three-note exercise from part one, but the second exercise will most certainly be harder this time, since there's more space between the notes. As always, play the exercises with perfect rhythmic accuracy, great dynamic contrast, and a smooth, musical feel, which can be especially challenging at very slow and very fast tempos.

The first exercise has an accented check pattern leading into the first four broken-up rhythms, played as accents, with all of the subdivisions filled in as taps. The key to playing this first exercise well is mastery and control over the four basic strokes (full, down, tap, and up). We've labeled the stroke type over each note (F = full, D = down, T = tap, and U = up).

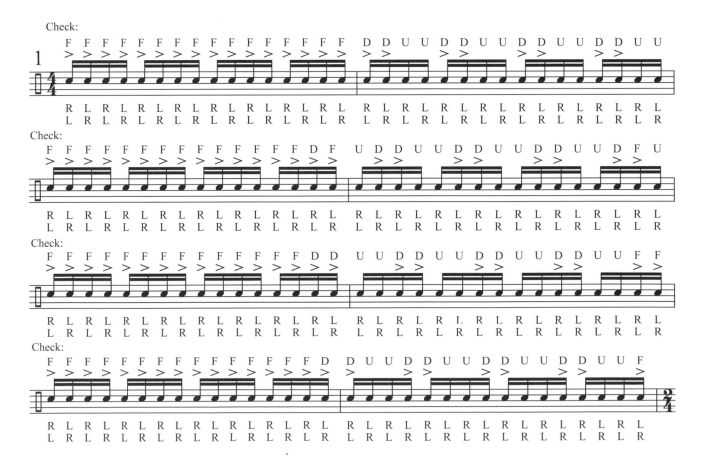

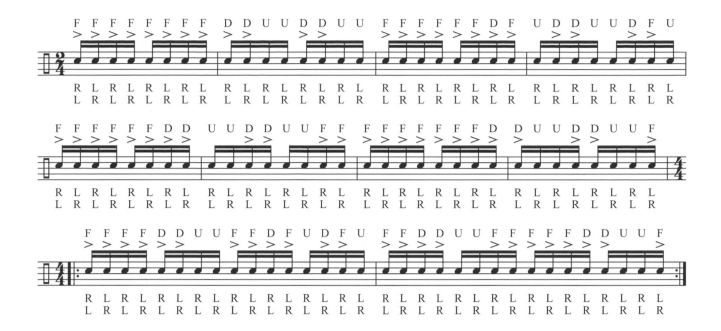

Here's a short exercise for the remaining pair of two-note groupings ("1-&" and "e-a"). Make sure not to stiffen up on the "e-a" hand. And don't let the counting and mental processing cause tension, which leads to dragging the tempo. Just trust your left hand to flow through, using relaxed free strokes. Go slowly, tap your foot, and repeat the exercise many times until it's comfortable.

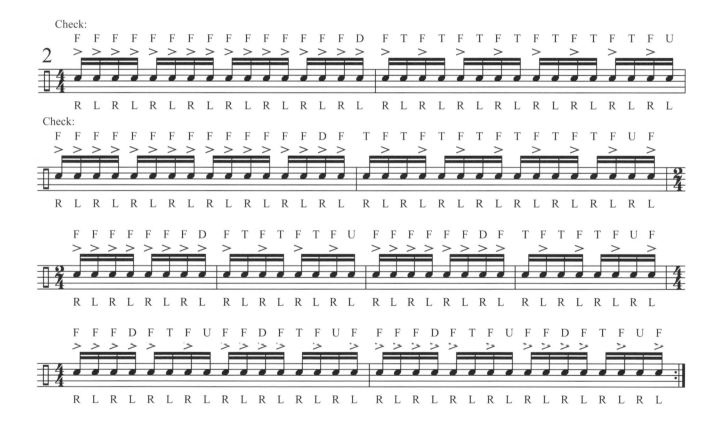

Now it's time to play the same exercises at one stick height, with the two-note groupings isolated. In most cases the check pattern flows right into the grouping rhythm, and the grouping rhythm transitions smoothly back into the check pattern. Use free strokes, and let the sticks glide naturally over the barline at those points. (Be sure to use the notated stickings.)

The hard part with these exercises will be keeping the rhythms accurate in the middle of the bar as you negotiate the space while your hands stop and start. Learn how to "play the space" in your head by subdividing the partials, which were played as taps in the first exercise.

I recommend playing these exercises in such a way that the free strokes flow up to the greatest stick height that is comfortable and easily sustainable. These continual, large motions will make the rhythms flow better, so use that to your advantage initially. Later, play the exercises at lower dynamic levels, where more finesse is required.

It's a good idea to play through the exercises on a regular basis. Just as with your more technical playing chops, your rhythmic perception needs to be trained and maintained. Plus, these exercises are downright therapeutic!

Rhythm and Timing

Part 3: Single 16ths

Let's focus on the four different single 16th-note partials, which are "1," "e," "&," and "a." Playing just one note may seem simple, but it can be quite a challenge to isolate "e" and "a" and play them accurately and in the pocket where they feel great.

The exercises will focus first on playing the single 16th notes as accents among taps. Then we'll move on to playing the rhythms with the spaces between them left open. The exercise with the accents and taps won't be too challenging to read, but it can be difficult to play using the perfect stick heights. Strive for high, strong accents and low, light taps, and make sure they are perfectly matched between the hands.

The second exercise will be more challenging, as there's a lot of space between the notes, and there's a lot of starting and stopping of the sticks. Playing these exercises with perfect rhythmic accuracy, great dynamic contrast, and a smooth musical feel is deceptively hard, especially at very slow and very fast tempos.

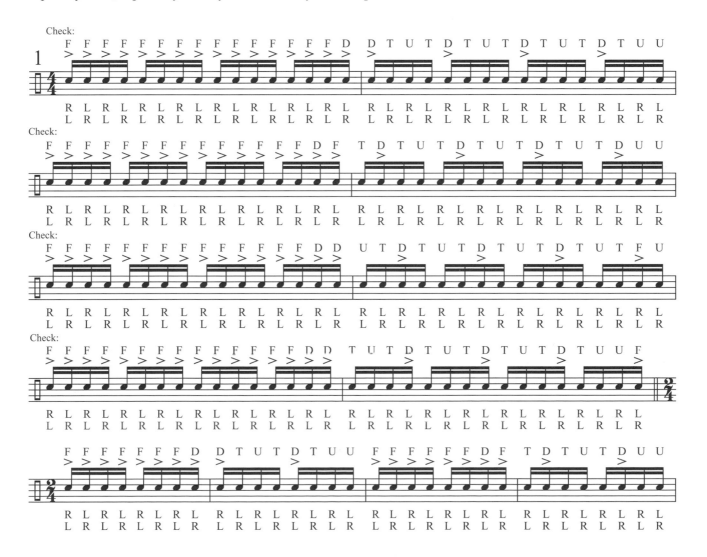

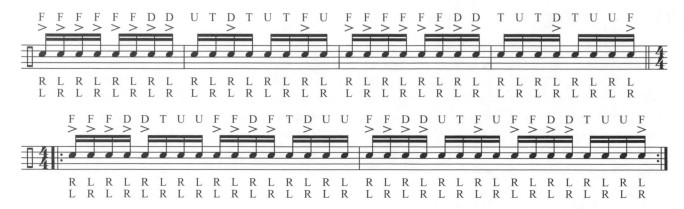

Now repeat the same concept without the taps placed between the one-note rhythms. The check pattern will flow directly into only the first two rhythms, and the two last rhythms will flow back into the check pattern. For those, simply let the sticks glide over the barline and land on the next note. The challenging part is negotiating the dead time between the rhythms, where you'll have to start and stop the stick at just the right time in order to play the next subdivision accurately and in the pocket. You have to learn how to "play the space" in your head by thinking of all of the 16th-note subdivisions.

At this point we've covered all of the possible one-, two-, and three-note 16th-note rhythms that occur within the space of a quarter note. Next we're going to shift to triplets.

Rhythm and Timing

Part 4: 8th-Note Triplets

Now we'll start working with 8th-note-triplet rhythms. Within the sets of three notes, we're first going to get into the three available two-note groupings. I've found that the best way to count triplets is "one-trip-let, two-trip-let, three-trip-let, four-trip-let." With that, the three possible two-note groupings are "one-trip," "two-trip," and so on. Then, when we move it back, there's a rest on the downbeat ("rest-trip-let"), and then it loops back around to "one-(rest)-let," "two-(rest)-let," and so on.

After those first three variations, we'll do separate exercises for the last two two-note groupings, which occur when you isolate every other 8th-note triplet over two counts. These end up being quarter-note triplets and upbeat quarter-note triplets. As usual, the exercises will focus first on the broken-up rhythms played as accents among taps, and then we'll play the same rhythms with the spaces in between left open.

Instead of a simple alternating sticking, we need to go with a natural sticking so that we can flow into and out of each check pattern. It may seem to be an unnecessary burden at first, but you'll be glad you learned the proper stickings, since they'll help you attain rhythmic accuracy as they flow into and out of the check patterns.

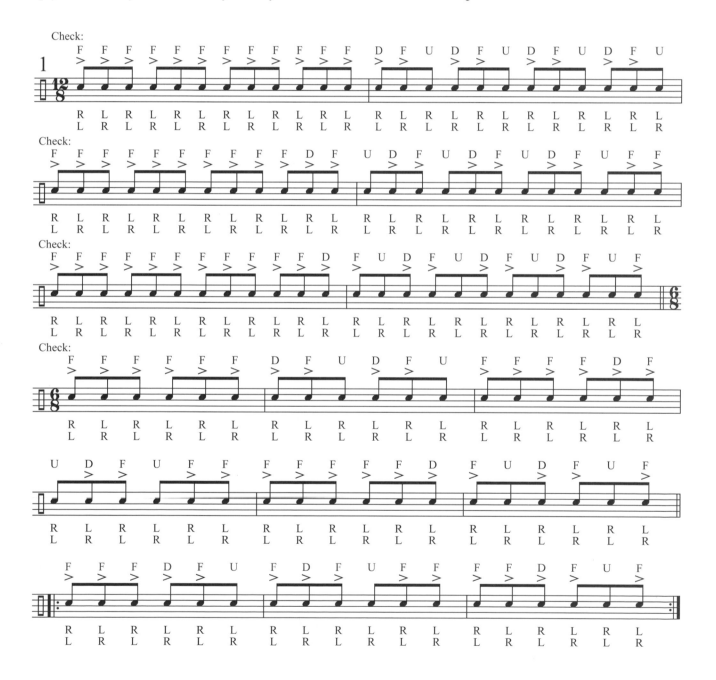

Here's a short exercise for the remaining two two-note groupings: the quarter-note triplet and the upbeat quarter-note triplet. Make sure not to stiffen up on the upbeat quarter-note triplets. Don't let the counting and mental processing grind you into tension, which leads to dragging the tempo. Just trust your hands to flow through with free strokes.

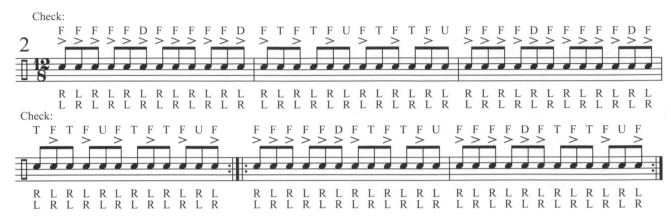

Next play those same exercises at one dynamic level/stick height with the rhythms isolated. The check patterns will flow into the first broken-up rhythm, and the last broken-up rhythm will flow back into the check pattern. Once your free strokes are flowing, let the sticks go over the barlines, as they will want to glide right into the next rhythm. The hard part will be keeping the rhythms accurate in the middle of the bar, as you negotiate the space while your hands stop and start. Learn how to play the space in your head by subdividing the partials that were played as taps in the first exercise.

I recommend playing this exercise with the free strokes flowing up to the greatest stick height that is comfortable and easily sustainable. There's rhythmic safety in having a continual, flowing motion, so use that to your advantage initially, and later play the exercises at a soft (piano) dynamic level, where more finesse is required.

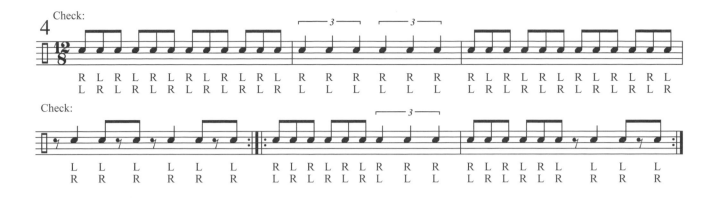

Rhythm and Timing

Part 5: Single 8th-Note Triplet Partials and Bonus Exercises

Here we're going to focus on the three different 8th-note triplet partials ("one-trip-let"). Playing on the downbeats is pretty simple, and the third partial isn't too strange, since we hear it all the time in swing and shuffle patterns. But isolating the middle beat of the triplet might start out feeling a bit awkward.

There's a lot of space between the three partials. The common tendencies are to rush/crush the space between the notes or to stiffen up and drag during more syncopated rhythms. It's very important to be able to feel each individual triplet partial comfortably, especially when you start playing quarter-note triplets and associated rhythms.

The exercises focus first on the partials played as accents among taps, and then the spaces in between are left open. Playing the correct sticking is crucial. The stickings will usually flow into and out of the check patterns, which makes it much easier to play with accuracy. Be sure to also practice the exercises with the left hand leading (opposite stickings), in order to help maintain balanced hands and develop confidence leading with either hand. Always use a metronome, and tap your foot. Count all of the played notes out loud, and then count just quarter notes out loud. Get in as many repetitions as it takes for these rhythms to feel natural. If you need to think about them, you have not yet fully programmed them into your musical vocabulary.

The first exercise has an accented check pattern leading into the three triplet partials played as accents among taps. The taps will guide the accented rhythms to their correct place. For maximum dynamic contrast and relaxed flow, be aware of which of the four basic stroke types (full, down, tap, and up) is being used. To help, we've labeled each stroke type over the notes (F = full, D = down, T = tap, and U = up). The exercise is in the 4-2-1 format, where you play four of each variation, then two, then one, and repeat it.

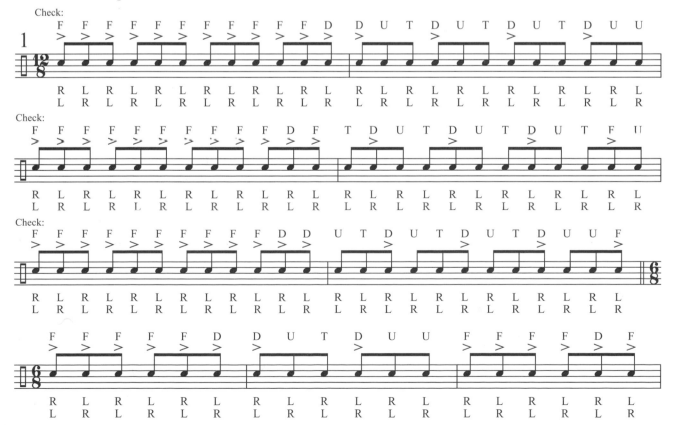

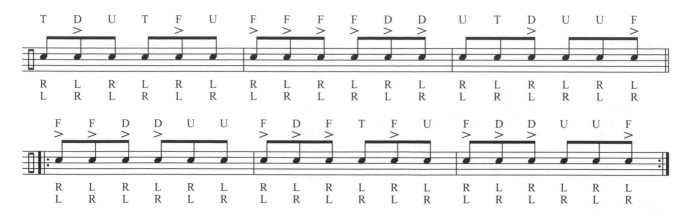

Now it's time to play the exercise at one dynamic level and stick height, with the rhythms isolated. Sometimes the check patterns will flow into and out of the broken-up rhythm, and sometimes not. Wherever applicable, let the sticks flow over the barline so that they glide into the next rhythm. The hard part will be keeping the rhythms accurate in the middle of the bar, where you have to negotiate the space while your hands stop and start. I recommend playing this exercise with the free strokes flowing up to the greatest stick height that is comfortable and sustainable. There's rhythmic safety in a continual, flowing motion, so use that to your advantage initially. Later, play the exercises at a lower dynamic level, where more finesse is required.

Here are two bonus accent/tap exercises that incorporate most of the rhythmic variations from the previous chapters. In addition to the rhythmic element, these make for a fantastic study in applying the four basic strokes. (We didn't indicate the stroke types in these, but feel free to write them in if necessary.) The first exercise is duple-based, and the second is triplet-based.

Hemiolas

Part 1: Introduction to Three Over Four

The word *hemiola* **has Greek roots** and means "containing one and a half," "half as much again," or "in the ratio of one and a half to one (3:2), as in musical sounds."

Three against two—or two against three—is nothing new when you think about the relationship of the downbeats in 6/8 versus 3/4. The two fit together mathematically, and you can go back and forth between them to change the feel quite easily. Below is an example of 2:3. Try singing the melody from *West Side Story*'s "America" along with it.

That polyrhythm is extremely useful and could turn into a study of its own, but I want to take the concept a step further and examine three-against-four and four-against-three groupings. If you add 16th-note subdivisions to the previous example, and turn the twos into fours, you can create a four-against-three pattern.

To turn the 4:3 pattern into a 3:4 pattern, change the time signature so that the three-note grouping is now outlining the pulse. (The group of four was outlining the pulse in the previous example.) In this context, the accents form a half-note triplet, or a 3:2 hemiola, in the second measure.

Now that we've defined the 3:2 hemiola, let's have some fun with these groupings of four notes within triplets. We're going to begin by having the first accent start at a different spot within the first grouping of four notes. It's crucial that you understand where the downbeats occur at all times. Don't allow yourself to detach from the pulse and just play the sticking/accent pattern in the hope that you land safely back on beat 1. In order for these rhythms to become useful musical vocabulary, you must understand your downbeat orientation every step of the way. Practice the exercises along with a metronome or recorded music, and be sure that you can comfortably tap your foot while counting quarter notes aloud.

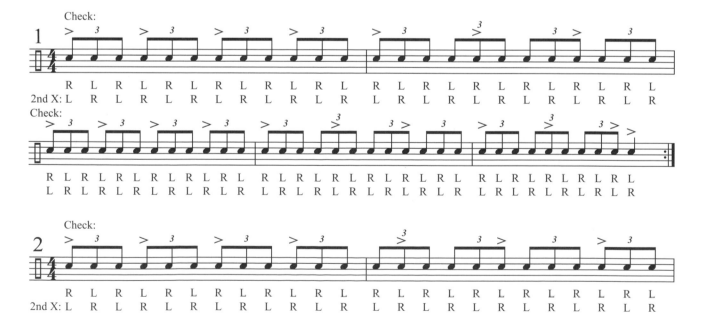

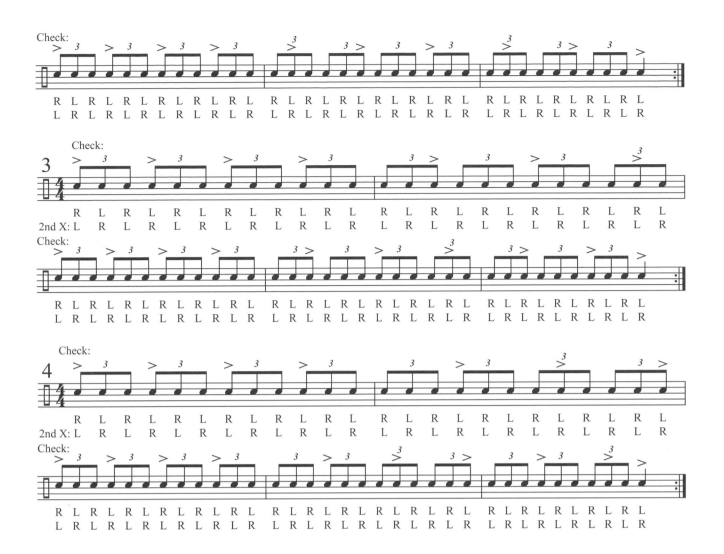

Now that we have some very useful accent patterns, it's time to add a couple of rudimental variations. While there are dozens of rudiments that we could impose upon these accent patterns, let's look at two very handy ones that use diddles.

First we'll add diddles to the accents. When playing the accented diddles, make sure that both beats of the diddle are accented. The first note will be a free stroke played mainly from the wrist, and the second stroke should be a downstroke played mainly from the fingers. Be sure not to attack the accented diddles too high or too hard, or you won't be able to match the second beat's velocity and volume with that of the first. The low taps should be played low and light and should favor finger control. Maximize the stick height and volume differential between the accents and the taps for the most musical contrast. Here's Example 1 played this way. Repeat the process with Examples 2–4.

Now we'll add diddles to the taps only. The accents should be played as strict downstrokes in order to bring down the stick height of the diddles for maximum dynamic contrast. Play the low diddles loosely, using finger control. I like to call this the drop/catch technique, where the hand drops the stick down for the first stroke and then catches it in the palm on the second. The process of catching the stick in the palm with the fingers adds some velocity to the second stroke, which helps it to match the first stroke dynamically. Repeat the process with Exercises 2–4.

You may be wondering: *How am I going to apply these hemiola patterns to the drumset?* There's the obvious option of orchestrating the patterns around the kit so that the accents are played on toms or cymbals. But the bigger picture is that if you understand these rhythms and can feel them naturally, new vocabulary based on them will develop spontaneously as you experiment on your own. The patterns can be used in short phrases for an unexpected rhythmic twist or in longer phrases where you want to trick the listener into a false downbeat orientation. (These types of extended phrases are what the fusion great Gavin Harrison calls rhythmic illusions.) A deeper understanding of progressively more complex rhythms will lead you to more creative and more musical ideas, which is always a good thing.

Hemiolas

Part 2: Accenting Three Over Four

We're going to add another accent to the half-note-triplet patterns. Previously we accented one note within three groupings of four 8th-note triplets, and then we shifted the accent to each of the four different positions. This time we're going to accent two adjacent notes within each set of four and then shift those to the four different positions.

I can't stress enough just how important it is to understand the relation of the quarter-note pulse to these accent patterns. Don't detach from the pulse and simply hope that you land on the next downbeat. Keep track of where you are in the measure at all times, so that these ideas can become a part of your vocabulary.

On a technical note, the four basic strokes (full, down, tap, and up) must be implemented for you to get good dynamic contrast between the accents and taps. The stroke types are indicated above the notes (F = full, D = down, T = tap, and U = up). Be sure to control the rebound on the downstrokes so that the sticks stop low to the drum and point down. This ensures that you're ready to play the following low and relaxed taps or upstrokes with some finger control. Be sure to squeeze the sticks on the downstrokes for only a split second after hitting the drum, and make sure the other three stroke types are played in a relaxed manner, with the sticks feeling heavy and resonating freely within your hands. Practice these exercises along with a metronome or music, and make sure you can comfortably tap your foot and count the quarter notes aloud while playing through the exercises.

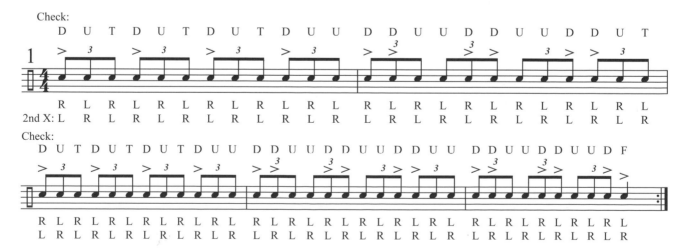

Now we're going to add roll variations to the exercise. First we'll add diddles to the accents, and then we'll roll all of the low taps. Repeat the process with Exercises 2–4.

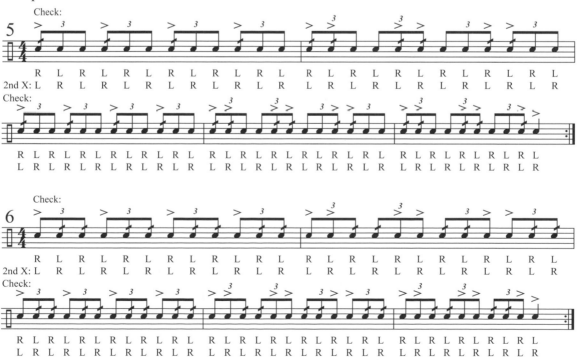

These rhythms, once you're comfortable with them, should spawn all kinds of ideas. If you have to think, count, or do any math while playing the hemiolas, then they're not ingrained in your rhythmic vocabulary well enough to spontaneously flow into your creative process. After many perfect repetitions, they will start to feel more natural.

Hemiolas

Part 3: More Three Over Four Accents

Now we're going to add yet another accent to the half-note-triplet patterns we covered in parts one and two. Part one had one accented note within the three groupings of four 8th-note triplets, and part two had two adjacent notes accented within the triplets. Now we'll accent three adjacent notes and move them to the four different starting positions.

As always, it's imperative that you understand the relation of the quarter-note pulse to these accent patterns every step of the way. Only once you've internalized the rhythms to the point where you can comfortably count quarter notes out loud and groove to them will they be of any use in a musical situation.

Since the accents now outnumber the taps, you will be using more loose, rebounding free strokes (or full strokes) than in the previous parts. When you're accenting three notes within a four-note grouping, one hand will need to play continuous free strokes while the other plays alternating downstrokes and upstrokes. It's crucial that the hand playing continuous free strokes does so with a natural flow—no extra tension! At the same time, it's important that the hand playing the upstroke/downstroke combination plays an accent that matches the other hand in terms of stick height and velocity, and that the tap is played low and lightly for maximum contrast. Don't average out the stick heights, the stroke velocity, or the amount of squeezing between the two hands. The downstroke must be played strictly, with a brief moment of squeezing, while all of the other notes are played as loosely as possible. Take your time to learn each pattern very slowly, and pay careful attention to the stroke type noted above each note (F = full, D = down, T = tap, and U = up). Practice the exercises along with a metronome or recorded music, and make sure that you can comfortably tap your foot and count quarter notes out loud while playing.

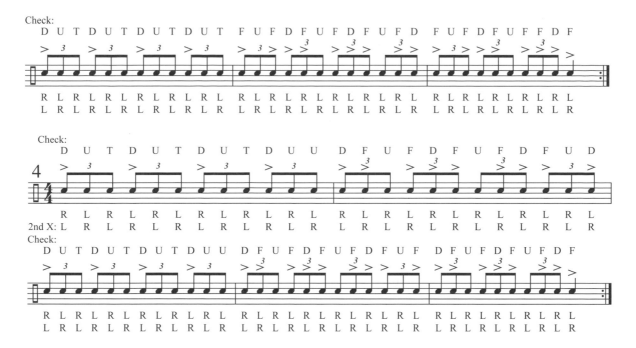

Next we'll explore roll variations, first by playing diddles (double strokes) on the accents and then by playing diddles on the low taps. Repeat the process with Exercises 2–4.

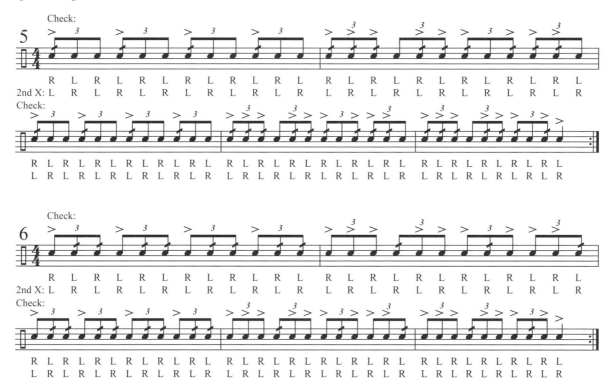

Mastering these hemiola accent patterns will do amazing things for your understanding of triplet partials. Triplet-based "rhythmic Illusions" will no longer throw you off, plus your own vocabulary will have greatly expanded. Internalize the exercises through a massive number of perfect repetitions, and then don't be surprised when they show up in your own creative stream-of-consciousness explorations behind the kit.

Duple/Triple Single-Diddle Gear Shifters

Part 1: 8th-Note Triplets and 16ths

In the next two chapters we're going to isolate our timing and sticking "gear shifts" between 8th-note triplets (twelve notes per measure) and 16th notes (sixteen notes per measure). Not only will these exercises be great for your hand technique as you develop the stickings and transitions, but they will also help solidify your timing as you transition back and forth from grooves and fills based on triplets and 8ths or 16ths.

With singles and doubles as our two stickings, there are four different possibilities using triplet and 8th-note metric rates.

You can have both note rates played with single strokes, or the triplets can be played with single strokes while the 16th notes are played with double strokes; the triplets can be played with double strokes while the 16th notes are played with single strokes; or both note rates can be played with double strokes. The exercises will all be in the "4-2-1" format, where you play four counts of each variation, then two counts of each (repeated), and finally one of each four times. You should also play all four variations in the reverse order.

It's imperative to practice these exercises with a metronome, tap your foot, and count quarter notes out loud so that the relationship between the patterns and the pulse is programmed accurately. Avoid morphing from one rhythm to the next; make the metric changes as concise and accurate with the metronome as possible. You may find that as you go from the slower rhythm to the faster one, it feels as if you have to delay the attack in order to give the last note of the slower rate its full value.

The exercises will do wonders for your comfort and accuracy in negotiating rhythmic gear shifts behind the drumkit, even if you never use these exact stickings.

Variation 1: Triplet Singles/16th-Note Singles
These should be played as free strokes where you dribble the sticks. Try to maintain a consistent stick height/dynamic level throughout. You may find yourself using the fingers more for the 16th notes and the wrists more for the triplets. This is fine; just keep the transitions smooth and concise along with the metronome.

Now reverse the order of the two components.

Variation 2: Triplet Singles/16th-Note Doubles
The triplet singles should be played as free strokes, while the 16th-note doubles will require what I call the "alley-oop" technique, where the first stroke is primarily played with the wrist and the second stroke is primarily played with the fingers. At faster tempos it's a good idea to add some forearm pumping on the doubles in order to avoid straining the wrists. Try to maintain one consistent stick height/dynamic level throughout. As always, try to bury the metronome on every downbeat for rhythmic accuracy.

Now reverse the order of the two components.

Variation 3: Triplet Doubles/16th-Note Singles

Now that the triplets are being played as double strokes, you will run into some real challenges with the stickings in the two-count and one-count variations. Take your time, and go nice and slow so you can really nail the transitions and so you have time to think about what type of stroke is coming next for each hand. Try to maintain relative matching stick heights/ dynamic levels throughout.

Now reverse the order of the two components.

Variation 4: Triplet Doubles/16th-Note Doubles

The double strokes at both metric rates will require the alley-oop technique, but the ratio of wrist to fingers will be different. The faster 16th-note doubles will also require more forearm pump and less wrist motion than the triplets as the tempo increases.

The trick is to transition from one to the next with clarity. Here more than in the other variations, you may feel that you have to delay the attack of the faster note rate in order to play the rhythm accurately.

Now reverse the order of the two components.

If you get through all of those exercises comfortably and want to take it to the next level, add diddles to the single-stroke variations to double the note rate.

Duple/Triple Single-Diddle Gear Shifters

Part 2: 16th Notes and Sextuplets

Here we're going to isolate timing and sticking gear shifts between 16th notes and sextuplets (aka 16th-note triplets). These exercises are great for improving your hand technique as well as your timing. Using singles and doubles, we'll cycle through four applications of the two stickings and metric rates. We'll begin by playing both note rates as single strokes. Then the 16th notes will be played as single strokes while the sextuplets are phrased as double strokes. For the third variation, the 16ths will be played as double strokes and the sextuplets will be played as single strokes. The last application is to play both note rates as double strokes.

The exercises will be in the 4-2-1 format, where you play four counts of each variation, then two counts of each (repeated), and finally one count of each (repeated four times). We'll also play all four variations with the 16ths and sextuplets in reverse order.

Practice these exercises with a metronome, tap your foot, and count quarter or 8th notes out loud in order to accurately internalize your perception of the rhythms. Avoid morphing from one rhythm to the next—make the metric changes as concise and accurate with the metronome as possible. When the sextuplets are played as singles, try counting 8th notes, since they're the common thread between the sextuplets and the 16th notes. When the sextuplets are doubled, it's best to think of the 8th-note-triplet hand motion.

Variation 1: 16th-Note Singles/Sextuplet Singles
These should all be played as free strokes where you simply dribble the sticks. Try to maintain one consistent stick height and dynamic level throughout. You may find yourself using the fingers more on the sextuplets and the wrists more on the 16th notes. This is perfectly fine; just keep the transitions smooth and concise with the metronome. Count straight 8th notes out loud through this variation, as that's the common thread.

Now reverse the order of the two components.

Variation 2: 16th-Note Singles/Sextuplet Doubles

The 16th-note singles should be played as free strokes, and the sextuplet doubles will require the alley-oop technique, where the first stroke is primarily played with the wrist and the second stroke is primarily played with the fingers. At faster tempos, add some forearm pumping on the doubles in order to avoid straining the wrists. It's best to think of the 8th-note- triplet hand motion under the sextuplet doubles in order to avoid micromanaging too many subdivisions.

Now reverse the order of the two components.

Variation 3: 16th-Note Doubles/Sextuplet Singles

This is another variation where the 8th note is the common thread. Count 8th notes and use them as a checkpoint in the middle of each single-stroke sextuplet. Try to maintain relative matching stick heights and dynamic levels between the two components, and focus on playing as accurately as possible with the metronome.

Now reverse the order of the two components.

Variation 4: 16h-Note Doubles/Sextuplet Doubles

Since both metric rates are played as doubles in this exercise, they will require you to use the alley-oop technique in order to achieve a good-quality sound. But the ratio of wrist to fingers will be different between the two rates. Also, the faster sextuplet doubles will require more forearm pump and less wrist action than the 16th-note doubles. The trick is to transition from one to the next with clarity. In this exercise you may feel that you have to delay the attack of the faster note rate in order to play the rhythms accurately.

Now reverse the order of the two components.

If you're looking for ways to take these exercises to the next level, add some diddles to the single-stroke variations.

Triplet Gear Shifter

The 12-18-24 Exercise, Part 1

We're going to challenge your hands by playing triplets as 12th notes, 18th notes, and 24th notes, with and without accents. (We'll use two other stickings in the next chapter.)

First let's define these rhythms. The 12th notes are simply 8th-note triplets (there are twelve in a bar of 4/4). The 18th notes, or "nine-lets," are a polyrhythm comprising triplets played over two quarter-note triplets. (The two "nine-lets" equal eighteen notes to the bar). The 24th notes are 16th-note triplets (sextuplets).

The four variations we're playing in these two lessons have their inherent challenges. Each requires modifications in technique, stick height, and touch. I normally avoid metronome markings in lessons so that students can choose tempos that work best for them. But for the purpose of describing the different techniques required here, I'll use 120 bpm as a reference.

While the exercises are short and seemingly simple, they can be quite difficult to play perfectly and will program a lot of very useful technique and muscle memory that can be applied in many different areas of drumming.

Variation 1 is played as straight single strokes. Each stroke should be a free stroke where the stick rebounds on its own to the same height as where it started. Never pick up the stick or let the back of the stick touch the inside of the hand (both are signs of extra work and tension in the hands). The sticks should feel heavy and resonate with a loud, high pitch as you dribble them.

The 12th notes should be played with an almost pure wrist turn and a little help from the fingers. The 18th notes will require more fingers, and the 24th notes will most likely have plenty of finger control involved. (Note that these wrist/finger ratios are not definitive formulas. Go with what's comfortable, and remember that more wrist equals bigger strokes, which equals more power.) Expect the stick heights and velocity into the drum to decrease incrementally as the note rates increase.

Make sure that you feel the opposite (non-leading) hand land confidently on beat 3 in the bar of 18th notes, and be careful not to round off the metric changes as you transfer from bar to bar. Also, don't cheat by adding mini accents to help you find the pulse. Try to make the rhythms feel smooth, and lock in with the metronome. You want to dribble the sticks at a uniform height without losing your place in the rhythms.

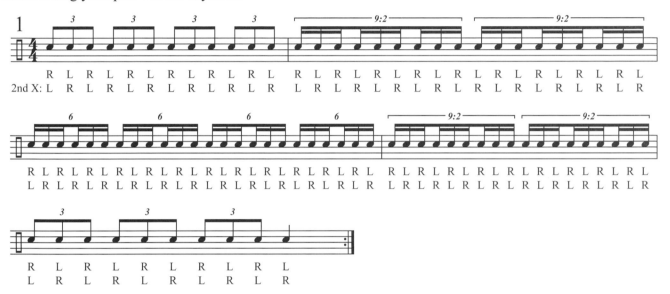

The following variation is the same rhythmically, but now we're adding accents to the beginning of each triplet. The 12th notes will use the four basic strokes (full/free, down, tap, and up). If you separate the hands, you'll find that each plays a repeating sequence of "down, tap, up." Interlaced, the alternating hands play "down, up, tap, down, up, tap."

The most important stroke to get right is the downstroke. Think of my catchphrase *downstrokes point down* in order to help you remember to stop the stick pointing down and low, right next to the drumhead. Doing that sets you up to play the following tap or upstroke relaxed and at a low height for maximum dynamic contrast. Avoid hitting the accents hard. Just let the stick's velocity from the higher starting point create the accent. All of the low notes (taps and upstrokes) should be played with relaxed hands, where the stick feels heavy and resonates freely.

The 18th notes will be played similarly to the 12th notes, but since there will be less time available to stop the stick low before initiating the following low tap, you'll need to compromise the downstrokes and the low stick height of the taps. (When there's less time to stop the stick, stop the stick less.) With this less strict variation of the downstroke, the fingers simply prevent the stick from rebounding all the way back up and allow some of the accent's energy to flow into the following tap. You may want to think of it as accents where the stick flops a little bit into the following tap.

For the 24th notes, there won't be enough time to use the wrist to lift the stick, so you will now have to compromise on the upstroke. To do this, use the Moeller whipping technique. Without writing a treatise on the Moeller technique (check out my book *Stick Technique* for that), the essential idea is that the stick is whipped from the forearm rather than played by the wrist. Here's the short explanation: Pick up the forearm while leaving the hand and stick hanging limply, and then throw down the forearm. This results in the hand and stick rotating up, relative to the forearm, for a split second before getting whipped down toward the drum at high velocity. You can also think of it as the forearm dragging the lazy hand and stick up before whipping the stick back down toward the drum. Make sure that the wrist stays completely relaxed. Any tension there will ruin the flow of the whip. After the accent, the stick will flop into the following tap, which is why I call this combination the Moeller whip-and-flop technique. The exercise is on the next page.

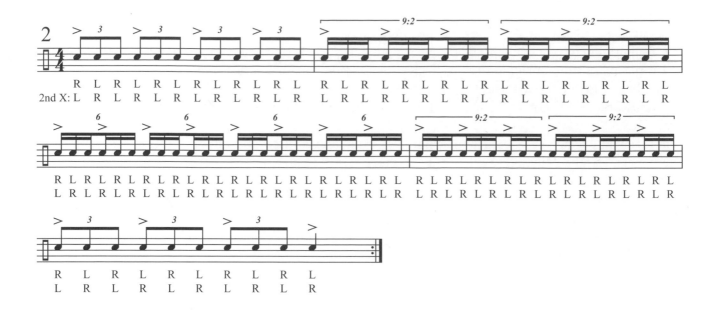

I suggest that you get in many repetitions of each subdivision, using the appropriate techniques, before practicing the entire exercise. This routine will pay dividends for the rest of your drumming life. Master it, and get ready to mix up the stickings in part two!

Triplet Gear-Shifter

The 12-18-24 Exercise, Part 2

Here we're going to apply two alternate stickings to the triplet gear-shifter exercise. To review, 12th notes are 8th-note triplets (twelve notes to a bar of 4/4). In the exercise, a bar of 12th notes is followed by a bar of 18th notes. The 18th notes ("nine-lets") are a polyrhythm where three strokes are played on each quarter-note triplet, totaling eighteen notes to a bar. The exercise concludes with a bar of 24th notes, which are known as 16th-note triplets or sextuplets.

The two sticking variations we'll use are "puh-duh-duh" (Rll) and "duh-duh-puh" (Rrl). These funny names, which are onomatopoeia for how the stickings sound, are commonly used by rudimental drummers. The different speeds of the triplets will require modifications in technique, stick height, and touch, and shifting gears from one rate to the next will require a lot of control.

I normally avoid metronome markings intentionally, so that drummers will go as fast or as slow as is comfortable. But for the purpose of describing the different techniques required in this exercise, I'll use 120 bpm as a reference.

The triplet gear-shifter isn't a long or complex exercise, but the key to developing great mechanics and muscle memory is playing thousands of perfect repetitions in bite-size pieces. The "puh-duh-duh" sticking consists of a right-hand accent followed by two left-hand taps. When the 12th notes are played in an average tempo range, the technique will be very simple. The accents can be played as free strokes that rebound back up or as downstrokes where you stop the stick low and close to the head. The two left taps require a little bit of finger control so you can play them as a "drop catch" diddle. In the drop-catch technique, the first stroke is played from the wrist so that the hand and stick seemingly drop toward the head. The second stroke is played by catching the butt end of the stick in the palm. The catch adds a bit of velocity to the second stroke, which helps to balance it dynamically with the first note.

The 18th notes will require the leading hand to play the accents as free strokes, so that the stick rebounds smoothly, while the low diddles will have to be played using an exaggerated drop-catch technique.

With the 24th notes, the accents will be played the same way, but you'll need to add a pumping forearm motion to play the diddles, since the wrist would otherwise be strained. Often, the 18th- and 24th-note diddles tend to come in late, so make sure to initiate the doubles right after the accent in order to keep the rhythm smooth and even.

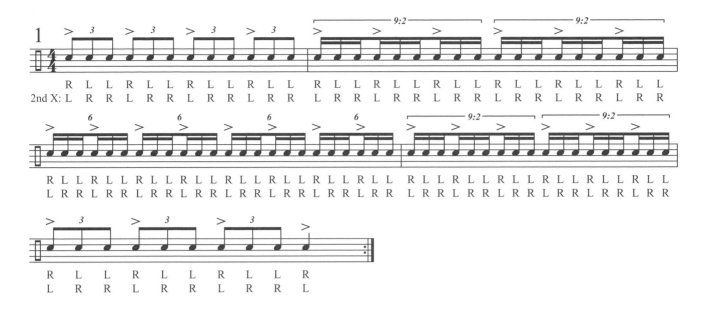

The following variation uses the "duh-duh-puh" sticking (RRL). This presents its own challenges, as it puts the accent at the beginning of the diddle. Using the four basic strokes, (full, down, tap, and up), you'll find that the hands play "down, up, tap" in succession. When playing the 12th notes, there's enough time after the accent to stop the stick low for the following tap. Making the stick freeze so that it points down towards the drumhead for a split second will set you up to play a relaxed upstroke at a low stick height. This creates you maximum dynamic contrast. After the right hand's first two beats, the left hand simply plays a relaxed low tap.

When playing the 18th notes, there will not be enough time to stop the stick low, so you'll need to compromise on the strictness of the downstrokes. Instead of stopping the stick, squelch some of the rebound in order to set you up at a lower (but not all the way down) stick height. I call this the "no-chop flop-and-drop" technique. This is a less strict variation of the downstroke where the fingers simply prevent the stick from rebounding all the way back up but allow some of the accent's energy to flow into the following tap. You might want to think of this technique as accents where the stick flops a little bit into the following tap. Flowing out of the accent requires finesse, so you can't hit the accent hard. But maintain a high stick height in order to maximize the dynamic contrast between the accent and the tap.

The 24th notes will be played very similarly, but you'll need to add a pumping forearm motion to play the first two diddles, otherwise the wrist would get strained.

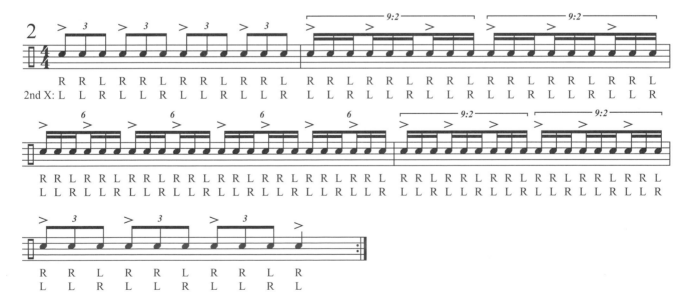

Get in many repetitions of each measure, using the appropriate technique, before putting together the complete exercise. Make sure that your rhythms are precise. The results of practicing all four variations will pay dividends for the rest of your drumming life.

Upbeat Triplets

Breaking Free From the Downbeat

Let's look at quarter- and 8th-note-triplet rhythms that are offset to the upbeats. When we talk about upbeats, we're usually referring to the "&" counts between the quarter notes in a straight 8th or swung context. In the following exercises we'll start triplets on upbeats instead of the usual downbeats. These upbeat triplet rhythms can open up new worlds of creativity, yet they're not so far out that they'll lose the average listener.

We'll start with exercises that focus on upbeat quarter-note triplets. If you play a bar of 8th-note triplets and accent every other note, the accent pattern will be quarter-note triplets. If you accent every other beat starting on the second note of the triplet, the accent pattern will be upbeat quarter-note triplets. Here are those rhythms, with a check pattern in between.

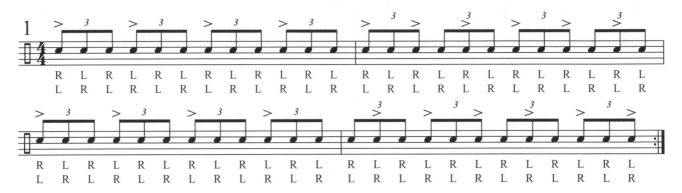

Now play the same thing, but drop out the inner beats. This gives you quarter-note triplets and upbeat quarter-note triplets in their pure form.

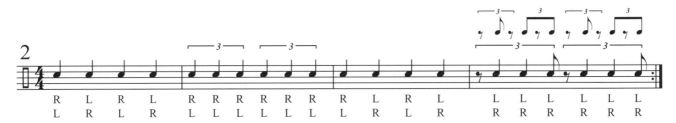

A great example of upbeat triplets within a groove can be heard in the Tears for Fears song "Everybody Wants to Rule the World." The hi-hat accent pattern consists of upbeat triplets set against a standard 6/8 groove. You can think of 6/8 time as 2/4 with a triplet feel, so there are two ways to count the hi-hat pattern (accents are in all caps): "one-TWO-three-FOUR-five-SIX" and "one-TRIP-let, TWO-trip-LET." The groove looks like this.

Now we're going to take things to the next level with upbeat 8th-note triplets. If you play a bar of sextuplets (aka 16th-note triplets) and accent every other note, the accent pattern will be 8th-note triplets. If you accent every other beat starting on the second 8th note of the triplet, the accent pattern will be upbeat 8th-note triplets. Here are those rhythms, with a check pattern in between.

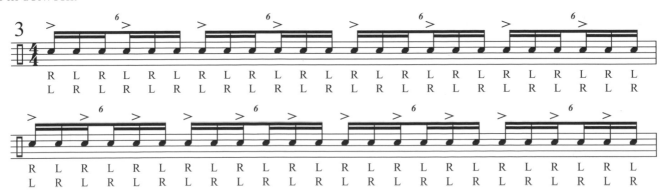

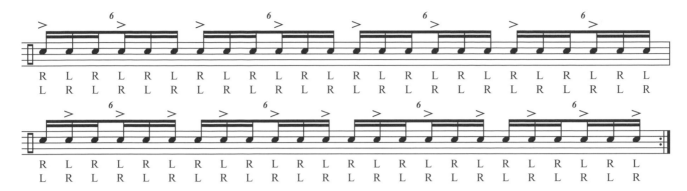

Now play the same thing, but drop out the inner beats. This gives you 8th-note triplets and upbeat 8th-note triplets in their pure form.

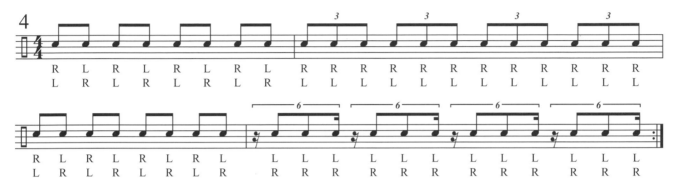

Finally, let's put some isolated upbeat 8th-note triplets into a straight 8th-note context. If we play the upbeat triplets starting on the "&" of beat 1, it'll look like the following.

Here's a fun exercise where the 8th-note triplet shifts from one partial to the next until we're back where we started. We've written the exercise using simple 8th-note-triplet groupings, even when they start on the upbeats (with the exception of when the triplets overlap beats 1 and 3). Try to play smooth triplets from one upbeat to the next without micromanaging each 16th-note partial.

With all of these exercises, be sure to play with a metronome and tap your foot. You should also try counting quarter notes out loud through the exercises. If you can keep your counting smooth, then you've proved that you're feeling the rhythms naturally. Once these patterns become part of your vocabulary, it'll be fun to see how they manifest themselves on the kit.

Quintuplets

Part 1: The Basics

Some may think of quintuplets—groups of five notes in the space of a quarter note—as an unusual rhythm reserved for the technical folks playing math music. But quintuplets aren't that different from triplets (which weren't always commonplace), and it's possible for us to use them in musical ways to increase our vocabulary.

There are resources that dig deep into using the partials of quintuplets to create polyrhythms and such, but I want to focus on some practical applications of this rhythmic grouping. We will get better acquainted with quintuplets through accent patterns, and then we'll play them with familiar rhythms, so we'll learn to feel the transition into and out of quintuplets. After you work through these exercises, you should find that the quintuplet becomes part of your vocabulary, coming out naturally in different musical contexts.

First we'll play quintuplets and move around some accents within them. This is as much an accent/tap technique builder as it is a chance to get comfortable with the feel of the five-note rhythm. The four basic strokes (full, down, tap, and up) are notated above each note with an F, D, T, or U, respectively. Start very slowly with each individual pattern, making sure that the stroke types are played correctly; the accents should be played at a nearly vertical stick height, and the taps should be played about 4" from the drum. Once each pattern is feeling comfortable, you can then string them together. Be sure to use your metronome or play along with music you like at an appropriate tempo, and tap your foot.

The first quintuplet accent/tap exercise adds a second accent that moves back one partial at a time.

The second exercise adds accents one partial at a time until all are accented.

Now try some exercises that put the quintuplets into a rhythmic context so you can develop the feel of transitioning into and out of them. Listen very carefully to the metronome, and make sure you're right with it. Play each phrase over and over until it feels completely comfortable, and then string the phrases together. Don't just practice until you get the exercise right once; practice until you can't get it wrong!

Quintuplets

Part 2: Polyrhythms With Fives

In this lesson we'll superimpose quintuplets across two beats using a five-over-two polyrhythm and across three beats using a five-over-three polyrhythm. These exercises can seem daunting, but once you get a feel for their sound, they'll become part of your vocabulary and will flow out of you musically on a whim. Remember: It's music, not math!

As always, use your metronome, tap your foot, and count the rhythms out loud, making sure the downbeats line up perfectly. Try counting quarter notes as you play. Once you're comfortable and the rhythms feel smooth, you'll have much more to say behind the kit.

First we'll look at a five-over-two grouping, or five notes superimposed over two beats. If we start with standard quintuplets (five partials to one beat) and accent every other note, the resulting accented rhythm is a five-over-two polyrhythm. In Exercise 1, we'll do this and gradually drop the unaccented notes in order to play only the five-over-two rhythm. Follow the sticking closely so that you flow smoothly into the polyrhythm.

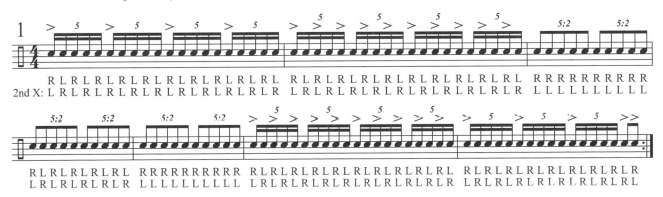

Next, to get comfortable with transitions, we'll insert the five-over-two phrase into an exercise using familiar rhythms. Avoid slurring or morphing the rhythms from one to the next, and make each transition staccato and concise.

Now we'll explore a five-over-three polyrhythm. We often use a common denominator as a reference with odd groupings, but in this case we'll have to just feel it, making sure each group of five starts at the desired place and is played evenly.

The first example will be in 6/8. Because 6/8 is generally felt with two pulses and a triplet feel, the polyrhythm might feel as though you're playing quintuplets on the downbeats. Set your metronome and tap your foot to the dotted quarter note.

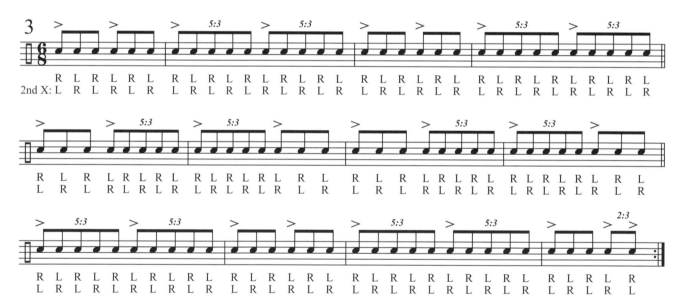

Now we'll do the same exercise in 3/4 time. The only thing that changes is where the beat is felt. Set your metronome and tap your foot on the quarter notes.

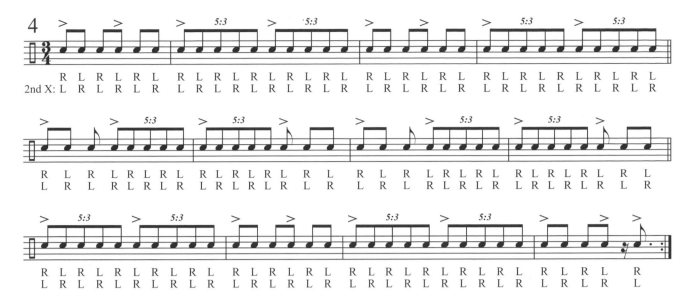

Next we'll insert the five-over-three polyrhythm into 4/4 time, using familiar rhythms to get comfortable with the transitions.

Chops Builders

Dynamics Mechanics

Loud, Soft, and Everything in Between

I believe that a drummer should be able to pick up sticks and make music on any sound source. The two biggest keys to doing this are having extensive rhythmic and rudimental vocabulary and employing excellent dynamic control. The more expressively you can play on one drum or cymbal, the more you'll be able to say when you add drums and cymbals. In this chapter we're going to explore dynamic changes and the mechanics necessary to modulate from one dynamic level to the next using crescendos and decrescendos. A crescendo is where we gradually increase in volume, and a decrescendo is the opposite. The exercises are pretty simple, but maximizing your dynamic expression within them will be a challenge and will require finesse and chops. The quieter you can keep your lower dynamics, the louder the loud dynamics will seem (and vice versa), so be sure to exaggerate the extremes.

The first exercise is an eight-on-a-hand variation called 8-8-16. Start low, at pianissimo (very soft), with the beads of the sticks just an inch off the drum. Then crescendo over one bar to forte (loud), until the sticks are turning as high as is comfortable relative to the tempo being played. (Don't overdo the heights at the louder dynamics.) The next bar will decrescendo in opposite fashion. The crescendo is the easier part, since you gradually interact with the stick less and let your fingers open up more in correlation with the increased wrist turn. The decrescendo is more difficult, since it requires more interaction with the sticks as the fingers close down in correlation with the reducing wrist turn. Be sure to watch your stick heights as they incrementally go up or down in correlation with the dynamics, and make sure that every stroke is a loose and rebounding free stroke. (Never tighten down on the sticks, regardless of the dynamic level.)

Now do the same exercise with the dynamics going down and up.

For more variation, try making the crescendos and decrescendos occur over only two counts and then over one count without changing the exercise. A lot of control is needed, as these dynamic changes will start coming at you very quickly.

Now apply the same concepts/techniques to a single-stroke-roll exercise using 8th and 16th notes. Here's what it looks like with the dynamics going up and then down.

Here's the reverse, with the dynamics going down and then up.

46

Once you have those down, try making the crescendos and decrescendos occur over two counts and then over one count without changing the exercise.

Now it's time to add dynamics to double-stroke rolls. These exercises will feel quite different from the previous ones, since rolls require downward pressure into the drum. The higher the dynamic, the more you'll have to dig in and use the fingers on the second stroke of each diddle. The lower dynamics require a lighter touch so that the rolls don't sound crushed. As you crescendo and decrescendo, your touch will have to gradually change in correlation with the stick height and dynamic level. Again, avoid playing too high or hard at the top dynamic levels, and make sure the dynamic of the second stroke of the diddle matches that of the first.

The exercise goes up and down in incrementally smaller phrases, from four bars to two bars, one bar, two counts, and then one count. Pace the rate of crescendos and decrescendos evenly over the entire phrase, watch the stick heights, and listen carefully. The check patterns are used to establish the hand motion and timing between rolls. Play the check patterns with a technique as similar to the roll as possible, with the exception of the forearm pump required to play rolls at faster tempos. The fingers should stay lightly wrapped around the stick while you play the check patterns, since at most tempos they don't open up very far for the diddles. Do this exercise in a straight-8th-note context, and then repeat it using triplets and triplet rolls. For extra variation, try also playing these with buzz rolls.

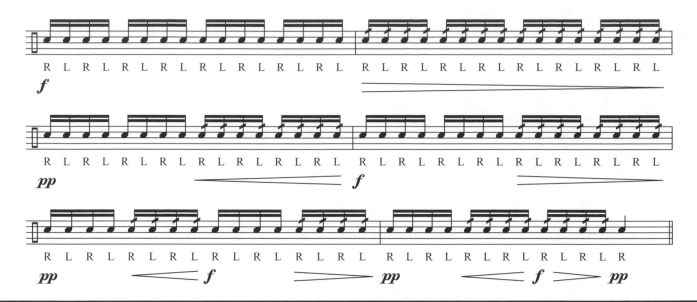

Fours and Sevens in 7/8

Part 1: Single Strokes

Here we're going to work on a couple of short-burst single-stroke rudiments: the single four and single seven. The key to executing these rudiments effectively is using finger control to play rapid free strokes. Single fours and sevens are very commonly used in fills on the drumkit, and practicing them on a pad will build speed and strength for playing doubles, triples, and even sets of four notes with each hand. As your finger control improves, these single-stroke bursts will become easy to play at very fast tempos. Speed certainly isn't everything, but the more musical options you have, the better.

Every stroke of the single four and single seven should be played as a free stroke. If the free stroke is rebounding properly, that means that each note is played with enough velocity down toward the drum to allow the stick to bounce back up, and that the wrist and fingers are relaxed so as not to inhibit the stick. It's also important that the fingers stay somewhat open and away from the palm. This allows the stick to vibrate freely and gives the fingers the opportunity to add a little bit more velocity to the strokes.

I recommend beginning at slow tempos, with the stick starting and stopping past vertical in order to ensure that the fingers are opening up to help move the stick instead of simply holding it, which would inhibit the speed and add unnecessary tension. If at any point the last stroke played by either hand doesn't rebound by itself, then you're practicing at a tempo that's too fast for your finger speed and you're not developing the desired finesse.

The exercise is in 7/8. The first bar can be broken down into groups of two, two, and three. The second bar repeats that pattern starting with the left hand. The third bar is reversed into groups of three, two, and two. The fourth bar is a repeat of bar three, except it has a triplet turnaround that allows you to repeat the exercise using the opposite sticking. Every group of two will contain a single four, and every group of three will contain a single seven. You could shorthand the four-bar exercise like this: 4-4-7, 4-4-7, 7-4-4, 7-4-turnaround.

The exercise is short, but don't be fooled. Developing hand technique is not about learning a lot of vocabulary; rather, it's about spending time getting in thousands of perfect repetitions to train your muscle memory. The muscle memory you'll develop through this short exercise will serve to make a lot of other things you play infinitely easier. Perform the exercise with a metronome, and be sure the strokes don't decrescendo (get softer) and that the last stroke in each hand rebounds all the way up by itself. Work up your finger control, and burn it!

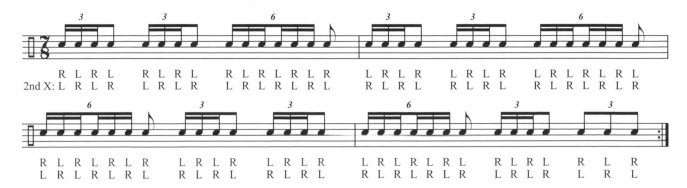

Fours and Sevens in 7/8

Part 2: Double Strokes

Now we're going to work on playing the Fours and Sevens in 7/8 exercise with double strokes. The key is developing the finger control to play well-balanced and even doubles. The rhythmic placement of the doubles in this exercise is very unusual, as many of the second strokes fall on 8th-note downbeats. Mastering the exercise will do wonders for the quality of your double strokes and help you build your rhythmic vocabulary.

When you play double strokes very slowly, both notes should be executed as identical free strokes, mainly from the wrist, with the fingers somewhat opened and away from the palm. Opening up the fingers a bit allows the stick to breathe and gives the fingers the opportunity to add a bit of additional velocity to the strokes. With the rebounding free-stroke technique, each note should be played with high velocity down toward the drum so that there's enough rebound to pop the stick all the way back up, and the wrist and fingers should be relaxed enough not to inhibit the rebound. I recommend beginning at slow tempos with the stick starting and stopping past vertical, in order to ensure that the fingers are opening up to play the stick instead of simply holding the stick, which would slow down the stroke and add unnecessary tension.

At medium tempos, you'll need to start using the alley-oop technique, in which the first free stroke is played mainly with the wrist and the second free stroke is played mainly with the fingers. Think of the first stroke as the setup throw and the second stroke as the slam dunk. The alley-oop technique in this medium tempo range can be played with two free strokes (where the second stroke rebounds on its own), or with a free stroke/downstroke combination, which is necessary at faster tempos.

At faster tempos, it becomes nearly impossible for the fingers to accelerate the second stroke and then get out of the way in order to allow the stick to rebound up. So at this point, the second stroke of each double will be played as a downstroke. The first stroke is a light stroke played mainly from the wrist and rebounds as the fingers open, and the second stroke is played mainly by the fingers as they squeeze the stick into the palm of the hand. The stick should hit the drum before it hits the palm, but the process of squeezing the stick into the palm also serves to add velocity to the second stroke so that it can be balanced with the first note. For downstrokes, I always recommend using the thumb to help hold down the front of the stick (if using an American grip) while the fingers pull the back of the stick into the palms.

Take the time to get in thousands of perfect repetitions in order to train your muscle memory. Play the exercise with a metronome, and always check that the double strokes are dynamically even and that every note speaks with equal power. Focus on being grounded to each of the seven 8th notes, regardless of whether it falls on the first or second beat of the double stroke.

Once you're playing the double-stroke version well, try linking it with the single-stroke version from the previous chapter. Focus on making the two versions sound as close to one another as possible.

Fours and Sevens in 7/8

Part 3: Triple Strokes

We're going to finish the Fours and Sevens in 7/8 exercise by playing it with triple strokes. As with double strokes, the key to playing high-quality triple strokes is finger control. The challenge is to play all three beats at equal volume, and you do that by using the fingers to add enough velocity that the second and third strokes are dynamically balanced with the first. Mastering this exercise will do wonders for your finger control and your triple strokes, which will show up in many contexts outside of the triple-stroke roll.

When you play the triple strokes in the exercise very slowly, all three notes should be executed as free strokes made mainly from the wrist, with the fingers opened up somewhat from the palm. Opening up the fingers allows the stick to breathe and gives the fingers the opportunity to add a bit of additional velocity to the strokes. Make sure that each stroke is played with high velocity down toward the drum, so that there's enough rebound for the stick to pop all the way back up. The wrist and fingers should be relaxed enough to avoid inhibiting the rebound.

At medium tempos, you'll need to start using the alley-oop-oop technique, where the first free stroke is played mainly with the wrist and the second and third free strokes are played mainly with the fingers. Think of the first wrist stroke as the setup throw and the second and third strokes as dribbles from the fingers. Immediately after playing the third stroke, the wrist and fingers should relax so that the stick can rebound up by itself. Remember that with free strokes we never pick up the stick— we only throw it down, just like dribbling a ball.

At faster tempos, it becomes nearly impossible for the fingers to accelerate all the way to the third stroke and then immediately let off in order to let the stick rebound up, so at this point the third stroke of each triple will be played as a downstroke. (It's also valuable to practice this faster tempo's technique slowly to develop accuracy.) Think of the first wrist stroke as the setup throw, the second as a dribble from the fingers, and the third as a slam-dunk from the fingers where the stick is pulled into the palm (aka "the brakes") and the thumb helps hold the front of the stick down when using an American grip. The process of squeezing the stick into the palm also serves to add velocity to the third stroke so that it can balance dynamically with the first. Just be sure that the stick hits the drum before you apply the brakes.

Take the time to get in thousands of perfect repetitions of this exercise to achieve the proper muscle memory. And be sure to use a metronome. I recommend beginning at slow tempos and having the stick start and stop past vertical in order to ensure that the fingers are opening up to play the stick instead of simply holding the stick and adding unnecessary tension. Check that the triple strokes don't decrescendo and that every note speaks with equal power. As you work yourself up to faster tempos, lock into the 8th-note primary stroke motion so you can feel the hands alternating 8th notes as they throw down the triple strokes. If you find yourself crushing the notes to where they start to sound like buzz strokes, lighten up the pressure into the drum and make sure you're not starting the first stroke too high or playing too hard, which makes it that much more difficult for the third stroke to match. I recommend playing this in American grip where the hands are at about a forty-five degree angle. This allows the thumbs to operate on the top-side of the stick where the thumb can help hold the stick down for the downstroke and facilitate finger control (like in French grip). American grip also gives you access to the palms to use as brakes.

Once you're playing this triple-stroke version well, try linking it up with the single- and double-stroke versions. Making them sound as close to the same as possible will most likely prove to be quite a challenge.

One-Two-Threes

Exercises for Finger Control

We're going to look at a hybrid rudiment called the "one-two-three" with a fun and challenging exercise that quickly warms you up and does wonders for finger control. In this rudiment, the right hand plays one note, the left plays two notes, and then the right plays three notes. Then the sticking is reversed before repeating the entire phrase. Playing three notes in a row with equal velocity can be challenging, but the biggest hurdle is finishing out the third stroke before transitioning almost immediately into the doubles as the sticking alternates. The one- and three-note groupings are accented, while the double strokes should be played as a low diddle. Here's the rudiment.

The first note should be played as a free stroke with a full rebound because of the accented three-note grouping that follows in that hand. The triple beats should be played as two free strokes followed by a downstroke. The last stroke of the three-note grouping should be a downstroke because of the two low diddles that follow, and at most tempos, all the fingers have left at that point is the ability to grab the stick into the palm. Be sure to practice these exercises extremely slowly and detail the accuracy with the stick heights via the four basic strokes (full, down, tap, and up). Here are the one-two-threes once again with the stroke types labeled.

Now we'll break this rudiment up and put it into an exercise. This may not look like much, but it's fun to play as it cycles around, and it can be challenging to play at even a medium tempo range. The first three bars are all the same as they alternate the leading hands, while the fourth bar serves as a turnaround. After those four bars, repeat the exercise with the opposite sticking until you're back at the beginning. Try to play all three beats of the triple stroke at the same volume (especially with the fingers as the tempo increases), and use the low alley-oop (or "drop/catch," wrist/finger combination) for the low diddles. Check that every isolated accent is played as a pure and loose free stroke (or full stroke), and keep your eyes on the beads of your sticks to define every note. I recommend starting this exercise as slow as 40–50 bpm so that you can truly define each stroke type. As you start to get faster, it helps to use the arms to initiate the double beat because the hand could be tapped out immediately after finishing the three-note grouping. Here's the exercise with the stroke types labeled.

Flowing Groupings and Fill-Ins

Exercises for Increased Single-Stroke Control

Next we're going to work on playing flowing groupings of notes with one hand while gradually filling in the spaces between the notes with the opposing hand. The leading hand will play groupings of two, three, four, and six notes, and each grouping will comprise an accent which flows into taps.

The key to mastering these exercises with maximum flow and speed is to train your mind to think about the two hands independently. Focusing solely on the lead hand will make it seem as if you can play twice as fast, since you're thinking about only half of the information.

At slow or medium tempos, the four basic strokes (full, down, tap, and up) will work just fine with these patterns. What I want to focus on here, however, is the technique required at faster tempos, which is the "no-chop flop-and-drop."

The no-chop flop-and-drop technique is used at faster tempos because there isn't enough time to stop the stick low after the accent to play the low taps. Instead, after executing the high accented note, the stick will simply flop and drop down to play the lower taps without stopping its motion. (When there's less time to stop the stick, stop the stick less.) Avoid using the fingers to add velocity to the taps after the accent, since you want the taps to be quieter than the accent. Though the flop-and-drop taps will not be as low to the drum as when you use basic downstrokes and taps, they will have a lighter sound because of their lesser velocity as they drop down in height. Since the taps flow out of the accent, don't hit the accent too hard, but be sure to start it from a high stick height in order to get the most energy out of it for the taps.

The secondary hand simply fills in the spaces with low taps. These taps should match the lead hand's taps as closely as possible, which means they might need to be played higher, lighter, and with more fingers than you would normally use when playing with regular taps.

It's helpful to play these exercises on different sound sources in order to focus on the flow of the leading hand. The lead hand shouldn't stiffen up when the secondary hand adds the tap fill-ins, or else you'll have an independence problem that will need to be worked out first. Try putting your pad on a couch cushion; play the lead hand on the pad and the fill-ins to either side on the cushion. This will require some side-to-side coordination as the hands alternate, but the goal is to be able to think of only the leading hand. Once you're comfortable, put both hands back on the pad without changing your mental approach. It's also a good idea to sing only the lead hand's part while both hands play.

Practice each pattern over and over with a metronome, or with music, at a stress-free tempo until it becomes second nature. Watch that the lead hand doesn't change as you alternate between the check pattern and the parts that include the fill-ins. With these patterns programmed into your muscle memory, you'll be surprised by how easily they'll resurface in your musical stream of consciousness.

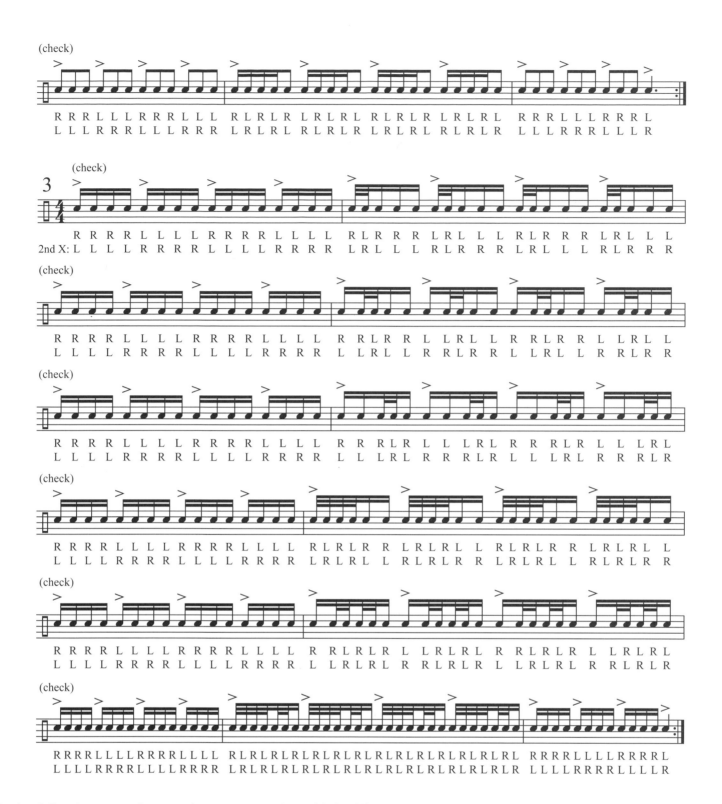

(check)

R R R L L L R R L L L L   R L R L R L R L R L   R L R L R L R L R L   R R R L L L L R R R L
L L L R R R L L L R R R   L R L R L R L R L R   L R L R L R L R L R   L L L R R R L L L L R

3

(check)

R R R L L L L R R R L L L L   R L R R L   L R L L   R L R R L L R L L
2nd X: L L L L R R R R L L L L R R R R   L R L L L R L R R L R L L L R L R R

(check)

R R R L L L L R R R R L L L L   R R L R R L L R L L R R L R R L L R L L
L L L L R R R R L L L L R R R R   L L R L L R R L R R L L R L L R R L R R

(check)

R R R L L L L R R R R L L L L   R R R L R L L L R L R R R L R L L L R L
L L L L R R R R L L L L R R R R   L L L R L R R R L R L L L R L R R R L R

(check)

R R R L L L L R R R R L L L L   R L R L R R L R L R L L R L R L R R L R L R L L
L L L L R R R R L L L L R R R R   L R L R L L R L R L R R L R L R L L R L R L R R

(check)

R R R L L L L R R R R L L L L   R R L R L R L L R L R L R R L R L R L L R L R L
L L L L R R R R L L L L R R R R   L L R L R L R R L R L R L L R L R L R R L R L R

(check)

R R R R L L L L R R R R L L L L   R L R L R L R L R L R L R L R L R L R L R L R L   R R R R L L L L R R R R L
L L L L R R R R L L L L R R R R   L R L R L R L R L R L R L R L R L R L R L R L R   L L L L R R R R L L L L R

In the following sextuplet exercises, I've opted to add the fill-ins from the front only, so as not to take up too much space. Feel free to explore the other possibilities on your own.

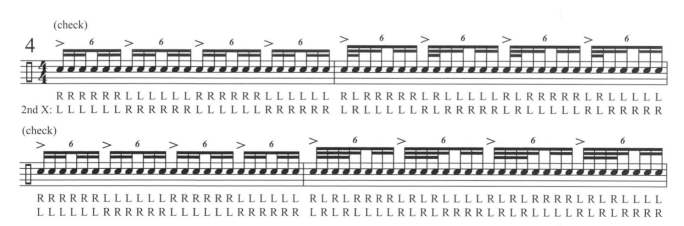

4

(check)

R R R R R L L L L L L R R R R R R L L L L L L   R L R R R R R L R L L L L L R L R R R R R L R L L L L L
2nd X: L L L L L R R R R R R L L L L L L R R R R R R   L R L L L L L R L R R R R R R L R L L L L L R L R R R R R

(check)

R R R R R L L L L L L R R R R R R L L L L L L   R L R L R R R R R L R L L L L L R L R L R R R R R L R L R L L L
L L L L L R R R R R R L L L L L L R R R R R R   L R L R L L L L L R L R R R R R R L R L R L L L L L R L R R R R R

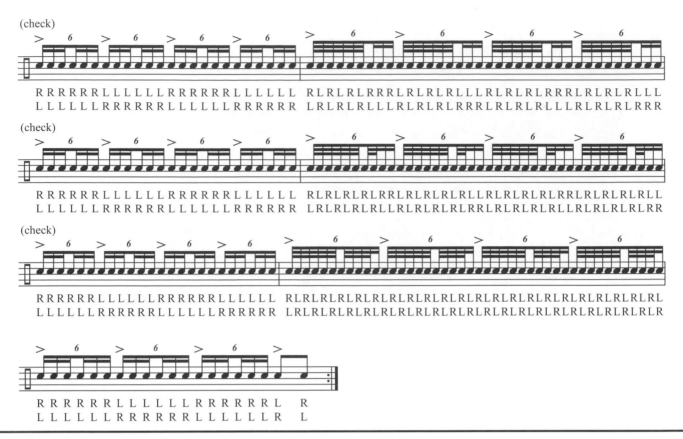

(check)

```
R R R R R L L L L L L R R R R R R L L L L L L    R L R L R L R R R L R L R L R L L L R L R L R L R R R L R L R L R L L L
L L L L L L R R R R R R L L L L L L R R R R R R    L R L R L R L L L R L R L R L R R R L R L R L R L L L R L R L R L R R R
```

(check)

```
R R R R R L L L L L L R R R R R R L L L L L L    R L R L R L R R R L R L R L R L R L L R L R L R L R L R R R L R L R L R L R L L
L L L L L L R R R R R R L L L L L L R R R R R R    L R L R L R L R L L R L R L R L R L R R R L R L R L R L R L L R L R L R L R L R R
```

(check)

```
R R R R R L L L L L L R R R R R R L L L L L L    R L R L R L R L R L R L R L R L R L R L R L R L R L R L R L R L R L R L R L R L
L L L L L L R R R R R R L L L L L L R R R R R R    L R L R L R L R L R L R L R L R L R L R L R L R L R L R L R L R L R L R L R L R
```

```
R R R R R L L L L L L R R R R R R L    R
L L L L L L R R R R R R L L L L L L R    L
```

Rudimental Clave With Inverted Stickings

Developing the Whip-and-Stop Technique

This fun and challenging exercise will do wonders for your Moeller-style whip-and-stop technique. The exercise uses the son clave rhythm as the accent pattern, with inverted stickings underneath it. The term *inverted*, in this instance, is borrowed from the inverted flam tap, and it basically means that the taps precede the accent. We're going to add flams, diddles, cheeses, and singles to the basic pattern for some fun rudimental variations.

As far as technique is concerned, the Moeller whip-and-stop motion will be the key. Since there's always a tap immediately before the accent, there's very little time for the wrist to perform an upstroke, especially as the tempo gets faster. In order to relieve the wrists, we'll replace the wrist motion with an arm motion. When you play the last tap before the accent, your forearm will quickly lift (leaving the relaxed hand and stick drooping down) and then quickly throw down to pass the hand and stick (leaving them pointing up), which whips the hand and stick toward the drum. This is the essence of the Moeller whip stroke, and it's how we're creating stick height for these exercises without employing the wrist. In fact, any engagement of the wrist muscles will slow down or completely kill the whip stroke.

The faster the up/down motion of the forearm, the less time it takes to generate the whipped accent stroke. And the farther up and down the arm moves, the bigger (and consequently louder) the whipped accent will be. Sometimes it will feel like an aggressive "herky-jerk" motion, requiring some work in the upper arms and shoulders to keep the hands relaxed. At fast tempos, it's more of an effect where the forearm throws down and the palm of the hand bumps the back of the stick down to seesaw the front of the stick higher. Since this technique is geared toward faster tempos, practice the exercises with mainly the fingers playing the taps, even at slower tempos.

The downstroke accent should stop as low to the drumhead and as quickly as possible. Think about making the downstrokes point down as you play on top of the stick at a steeper angle, where the thumb is higher than the bead. Not only should you use the back fingers to pull the stick into the palm to create the downstroke, but you should also use the thumb to push down on the front of the stick. By using American grip, with the thumb a bit more on the top than on the side, and by having no gap between the thumb and first finger, you can stop the stick quickly and with less tension. Stopping the stick quickly and low to the drum sets you up to initiate low, light taps. It's challenging enough to get big accents in a hurry, so don't lessen the dynamic contrast by playing the taps too high/loud. Even when practicing this exercise very slowly, be sure to use the faster tempo's technique with big whip-stroke accents and finger-stroke taps.

Now that we've covered the technique, let's take a look at the basic exercise:

```
R L L L R R R L    L L L R R L L L    L R R R L L L R    R R R L L R R R
```

Now add flams.

IRLL rLRRIRL LLrLRIRLLL rLRRIRLL rLR RRIRLrLRRR

Next, drop the flams and add diddles on the accents. When you accent diddles, both beats should be accented. (Here's where your free stroke/downstroke alley-oop finger control comes into play.) Avoid pressing down into the drum or attacking the diddles too hard. That will only cause you to crush the spacing between the notes, and it will leave the fingers with almost no opportunity to accent the second beat of the diddle.

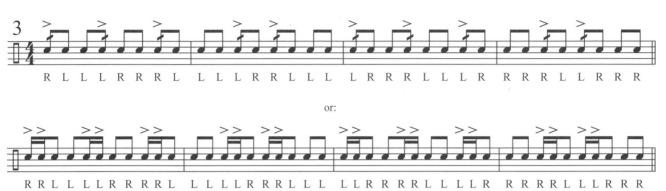

RLLLRRRL LLLLRRLLL LRRRLLLR RRRLLLRRR

or:

RRLLLLRRRL LLLLRRLLL LLRRRRLLLR RRRRLLLRRR

Now we'll combine the previous two variations in order to play cheeses on the accents. If you don't know what a "cheese" is, it's just a flam and a diddle combined.

IRLL rLRRIRL LLrLRIRLLL rLRRIRLL rLR RRIRLrLRRR

Finally, we'll work on our singles by dropping in some taps with the opposite hand. Think only about the lead hand when you play this variation, and don't let the coordination of the two hands stiffen you up or bog you down.

RLRLRLRLRLRLR LRLRLRLRLRLRLR LRLRLRLRLRLRL RLRLRLRLRLRLRL

Once you've worked through all of those variations, try stringing them together, or play the first example between each variation. When you work them up to 200 bpm, it may be easier to think of the rhythms as 16th and 32nd notes. As always, use your metronome, tap your foot, and watch your stick heights. Strive for maximum accent/tap contrast. Shut your wrists off, and whip it good!

Hemiola Shifter With Three Stickings

Exploring the Half-Note Triplet

Here we're going to play half-note-triplet hemiolas in four positions, with three different stickings. Each sticking will require a totally different technical approach and will have its own unique sound. For good measure, we'll also add some flams, which oddly enough can make the exercises *easier* to play.

The half-note triplet can be brought to light if you accent every fourth beat of a constant stream of 8th-note triplets. The accents will then shift to start at four different points within the first half-note-triplet's note value. It's important to practice these exercises with a metronome and to be able to count quarter notes out loud while playing them, to take out any guesswork as to where they fit within a steady pulse.

What we're working toward here is the ability to play these exercises with three stickings: alternating, inverted, and what I call "floppy flow." Alternating is simply right to left, while an inverted sticking is where the same hand plays the taps that precede the accents (the name is borrowed from the inverted flam tap rudiment). Floppy flow is a sticking where an accent is followed immediately by taps on the same hand. The accent flops and naturally decrescendos into lighter taps using the "no-chop flop-and-drop" technique. Floppy flow is used when there isn't enough time to play a strict downstroke with the stick stopping immediately at a low tap height.

The first exercise uses an alternating sticking. The four basic strokes (full, down, tap, and up) should be employed, and you should define your stick heights for maximum dynamic contrast. There's a check pattern of triplets with accents on the downbeats between each hemiola accent pattern to help you relate back to the quarter-note pulse. After the four patterns, the exercise repeats with the left hand leading.

Now we'll add flams to the accents. The tricky part is playing the low triple beats under the flam accent that's formed by the tap/grace note/tap combination. Finger control for the low triple beat should be used.

Now we'll use the inverted sticking where the taps precede the accent on the same hand. Since there's always a tap immediately before an accent, the wrist has very little time to perform an upstroke, especially as the tempo gets faster. In order to relieve the wrists, we'll replace the wrist motion with an arm motion. While playing the last tap before the accent, the forearm will quickly pick up, leaving the relaxed hand and the stick drooping down, and then quickly throw down to whip the hand and stick toward the drum. That's the essence of the Moeller whip stroke, and that's how in this application we're creating stick height without employing the wrists. It all happens in the blink of an eye, and as you get faster it will sometimes feel like an aggressive "herky jerk" motion requiring some work in the upper arms and shoulders to keep the hands relaxed.

In this version of the exercise, each pattern will be played off the right and left hand before you move on to the next pattern. Make sure that the downstrokes stop as low to the head as possible and that the low taps are light and relaxed using finger control.

Now let's add flams to that. This exercise may be easier to execute, as the flams will now help connect the hands when transitioning back and forth.

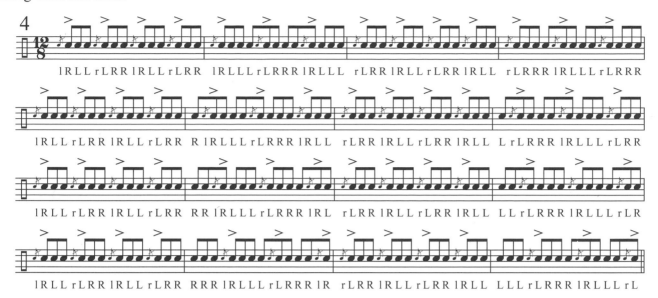

Now we'll play the exercise using the floppy-flow sticking and the "no-chop flop-and-drop" technique. Since the taps need to flow out of the accent, it's important not to hit the accent hard or restrict the stick's rebound any more than necessary. Use your fingers to steer the rhythms and maintain taps in longer phrases, but don't use them to add velocity or strength to the taps. You want to emulate the loud-to-soft accent/tap transition while letting go of strict downstroke control and stick-height differential. You can maximize the velocity of the accent stroke by starting with the stick in a vertical position or even beyond.

Finally, let's add flams. The challenge is to get consistent flam quality as you transition between the hands.

Pataflafla Builder

Developing a Challenging Yet Musical Rudiment

One of the most beneficial of the forty PAS rudiments is the pataflafla. It's one of the few where each hand plays a totally different part. The leading hand uses what I call the Moeller whip-and-stop technique, and the secondary hand uses what I call the no-chop flop-and-drop technique. Playing a rudiment with the weaker hand leading usually involves just a mental switch, but now there's a physical learning curve as well.

When you dissect the pataflafla, you'll find that the lead hand plays two low taps immediately preceding an accent. When you play the rudiment slowly, there's plenty of time to execute the three consecutive notes as a tap, upstroke, and downstroke, using the wrists. At a medium speed and up, there isn't enough time to play the upstroke without tension and/or a rhythmic gap before the accent, so we'll replace the wrist motion with a forearm motion: the Moeller whip stroke. After the accent, there's time to stop the stick low to the drum before starting the process over, so we'll call it the Moeller whip-and-stop motion.

These three consecutive notes will be played as follows. First, drop the hand and stick, with the fingers open, for the first tap. Lift the forearm, while allowing the hand to drop down, and let the stick bump the drum for the second tap. (We can call this a Moeller upstroke.) Finally, throw the forearm down, with the wrist limp, to create a whipped accent. Immediately after you play the accent, grab the stick so that it stops pointing down and right next to the drumhead. This sets you up to repeat the series of three notes starting from a low tap height. Practice the lead hand's motion slowly and with an exaggerated whipping technique.

The secondary hand plays "1-e-a, 2-e-a, 3-e-a, 4-e-a," with the accent on the "a." At slow tempos, playing a high accented note immediately followed by two low taps can work using a downstroke and two taps. But at medium tempos and up, there isn't enough time to stop the stick low after the accent and before the low taps. Here's where you'll have to employ the no-chop flop-and-drop motion so that the high accented note can be followed by lower and lighter taps without the stick stopping. I call it the no-chop flop-and-drop, since you want to avoid using the fingers to add velocity to the taps after the accent. The tap strokes will not be as low as usual, but they will sound light as they drop down in height sequentially. Since the taps flow out of the accent, you can't hit the accent hard. But be sure to attack the accent from a high stick height in order to get the most out of it.

In the exercise, we'll play pataflaflas with just the leading hand, then with both, then with just the secondary hand, and then with both again. It's a good idea to also play this with each hand on a different surface in order to make sure there's no change in the motion as the hands go from solo to coordinated. For an additional challenge, try counting each hand's part out loud.

Once you've mastered the pataflafla builder using right- and left-hand lead, you can move on to a 16th-note exercise where the rudiment gets scrambled around systematically. I've put the variations in the 4-2-1 format, where we play four counts of each variation, then two counts of each (and repeat), and then one count (repeat four times). Going into and out of the fourth pattern, you'll need to play three flams in a row. There, one hand will need to flow from the no-chop flop-and-drop technique immediately into the Moeller whip-and-stop technique.

Do your best to exaggerate the accents in both hands, practice with a metronome, and tap your foot so that you're rhythmically grounded. These exercises are challenging for the hands, and the skills you'll develop from them will have applications far beyond the practice pad.

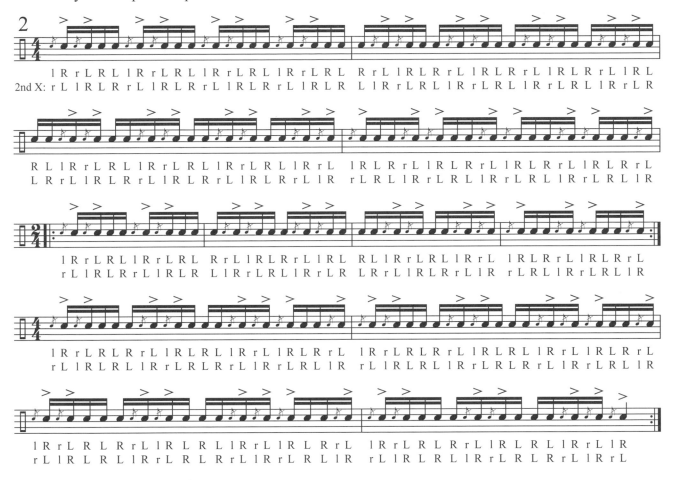

Pataflafla Hemiolas

Straight and Alternating Versions Over Half-Note Triplets

Now we're going to add the pataflafla (a rudiment consisting of two adjacent flams) to some two-accent hemiola patterns to give us a rhythmic and rudimental challenge. In its most basic form, a hemiola is a pattern based on the three-against-two polyrhythm that creates a new pulse over the original tempo.

For these exercises we'll use an accent pattern based on the half-note triplet. A half-note triplet is three half notes taking the place of two, so in the exercises there will be three half-note triplets played within a bar of 4/4 time. An easy way to uncover this rhythm is to play a bar of 8th-note triplets in 4/4 and accent every fourth note. If you then add a second accent adjacent to the first, you'll have the accent pattern that we're going to manipulate with flams. We will then shift these accent patterns to each of the four possible positions within one half-note triplet's note value.

The pataflafla consists of two adjacent accented flams. It's one of the more challenging rudiments, since each hand plays a different part and requires a different technical approach. As the pataflafla moves into the different rhythmic positions, the technical demands to play the flams will change. To negotiate the accented flams in these exercises at a medium tempo and up, you'll need to use all four methods of approaching accent/tap patterns, including the four basic strokes (full, down, tap, and up), the no-chop flop-and-drop, the Moeller whip-and-flop, and the Moeller whip-and-stop.

When there's time before the accent to prepare, via an upstroke, and there's time to stop the stick low to the drum afterward with no stress, the four basic strokes should be used. When there's time to prep for an accent, via the upstroke, but no time to stop the stick low after the accent for the following tap, the no-chop flop-and-drop technique should be used. When there's no time to prep for an accent using an upstroke via the wrist, the Moeller arm whip should be used to set up for the accent. If there's time to stop the stick after the whipped accent, use the Moeller whip-and-stop technique; if not, use the Moeller whip-and-flop. (For more on all of these methods, check out my book *Stick Technique*.)

When you play these exercises, it's very important to understand the relation of the quarter-note pulse to the accent patterns. Don't detach from the pulse and hope that you land on the next beat 1. To ensure that you're keeping the pulse accurately, practice these exercises along with a metronome or your favorite recordings, tap your foot, and count quarter notes out loud.

Here's the first version, which features the regular pataflafla and a check pattern consisting of flam accents.

For a rudimental challenge, try adding flam drags, cheeses (flam diddles), and flam fives (five-stroke rolls with a flam at the beginning) to the check pattern and on the second flam of each pataflafla. Note that sometimes you'll need to leave out the flam on beat 1 of the check pattern if you're coming off a diddle. You'll also have to leave out the diddle at the end of the flam-five variation in order to change hands.

Now let's try the second version, which contains alternating pataflaflas. You'll notice that, instead of doing each variation once and repeating the whole exercise with the left hand leading, now each pattern will be played with right- and left-hand lead before you move on to the next variation.

I R L R r L R L I R L R r L R L   I R L R r L r L R L I R I R L R r L

r L R L I R L R r L R L I R L R   r L R L I R I R L R r L r L R L I R

Finally, add flam drags, cheeses, and flam fives to the exercise.

Consecutive Flams

Part 1: Spaced Out

The next three chapters incorporate flams. All of these exercises will consist of single flams followed by sets of two, three, and four flams. Then we'll reverse the order to end up back where we started. There will be different flam placements and transitions to navigate, as well as some rudimental ornamentations for additional challenges. These are really fun to play, and your mind has to stay engaged as you cycle through the progression. These patterns also apply well to the drumkit if you place the unaccented notes on the snare while moving the accents around the toms and cymbals.

The exercises we're using this time have a tap played between each flam when there are sets of two flams or more, and flam accents are used to switch hands. This will make more sense after you have a look at the exercise.

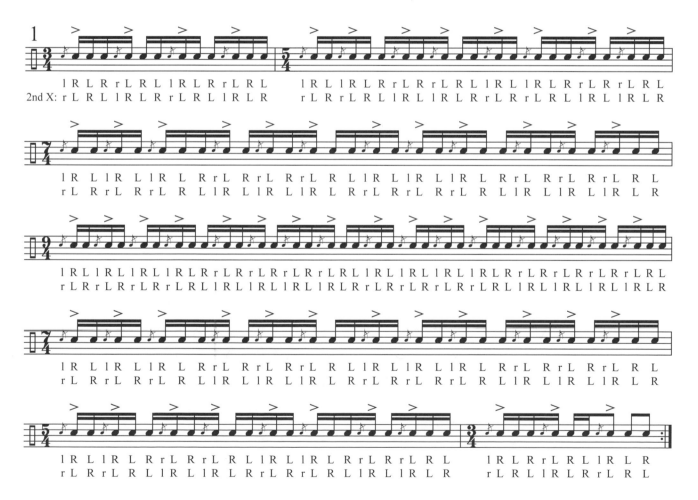

The two hands play distinctly different parts. One plays the accents, while the other plays a continuous stream of taps and grace notes. The accented hand plays a downstroke when there's only one flam, and a combination of free strokes and downstrokes when there's more than one accent in the series. (The last accent in a series will always be a downstroke, in order to set up the hand for the forthcoming low notes.) The real challenge lies in the low hand as it dribbles a smooth stream of grace notes and taps. This exercise will test your single-stroke control at low stick heights. Normally, grace notes are placed ahead of the primary note they're tied to and are played lower than taps. But in this situation there's no practical way to make quick rhythmic shifts and alter the stick heights, so all of these notes will flow evenly. The flams will be created by placing the accents just *behind* the grace notes. (The low hand is in charge!)

Make sure that the last accent per hand is played with a concise downstroke so that the stick freezes pointing down toward the drum. Doing this sets you up for a clean attack of low taps and grace notes.

To develop this exercise with accurate flow, rhythm, and feel, it's a good idea to separate the hands and isolate each section of the exercise. Try putting your practice pad on a quieter surface, such as a couch cushion, and then play the accents on the cushion and the inner beats (taps and grace notes) on the pad. Doing this will allow you to isolate and analyze the stream of low notes. When you play the exercise perfectly, you should hear low and even 16th notes on the pad.

From there, I like to use a four-part system to isolate the hands and develop control. First, play the pattern with both hands on the pad. Second, move the accents to the cushion. Third, air-drum the accents to either side of the pad. Finally, air-drum the accents directly over the playing area of the pad. (These are called ghost flams.) Repeat these steps, striving for a smooth flow of 16th notes on the pad that are unaffected by the accents.

While it makes perfect sense to think of each piece of the exercise in bite-size chunks, you'll be better off feeling the quarter-note pulse that runs throughout. Use your metronome, tap your foot, and count quarter notes out loud. Focus on making the "e" and "a" syncopations on either side of the quarter note feel comfortable.

Once you master the basic exercise, try adding rudimental variations such as flam drags, cheeses (flammed diddles), and flam fives (flammed five-stroke rolls). Whenever there's an accent on a diddle, make sure to accent both beats of the diddle and play them accurately—don't crush them.

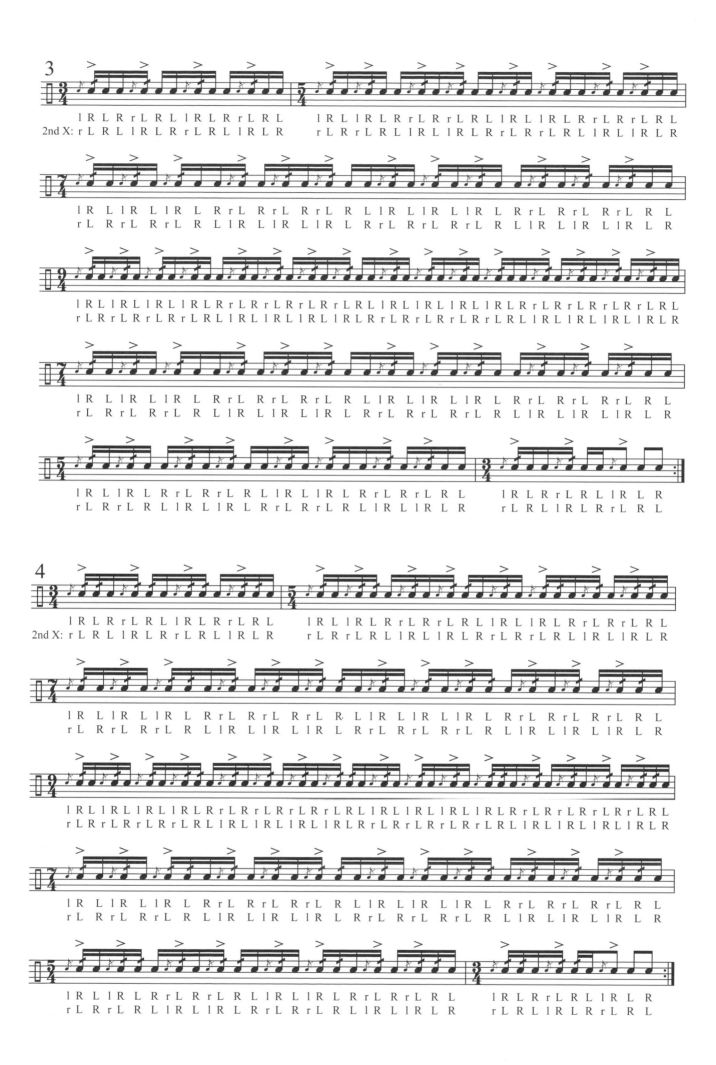

Consecutive Flams

Part 2: Adjacent

Let's take out the taps between the consecutive flams so that the flams are adjacent. When you do that, the challenge becomes playing the consecutive flams with consistent grace-note placement and sound quality. We'll still use the flam accent to transition from right- to left-hand lead. These patterns will do wonders for your control, and they sound great voiced around the drumkit.

Here's the exercise.

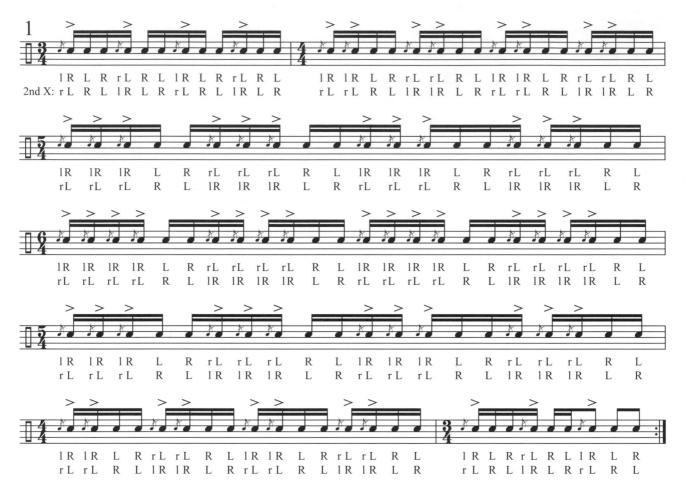

The hands play two distinctly different parts, and it's important to be able to think about them separately. The low hand playing the constant stream of taps and grace notes has to stay perfectly even and consistent, while the accent hand needs to play each accent with consistent power and volume. Since the accents are strung together, some finger control will be necessary to aid the wrists when they're playing the accents at faster tempos, so that the accents don't decrescendo.

Equally important is the downstroke control on the last accent in each series. When there's more than one accent, you must transition quickly from a free stroke to a downstroke. Try to stop the downstroke pointing down toward the drumhead so that the following stream of taps and grace notes can be initiated at a low stick height. The taps and grace notes must be played smoothly and evenly using finger control. These low, flowing notes dictate where the primary notes of the flams must be placed. The low hand is in charge! When the initial primary note of the flam is attacked accurately, the rest in the series generally follow suit. When the first flam is played flat or too wide, the rest of the flams will likely also be played with the same issue.

Here's the exercise with flam drags.

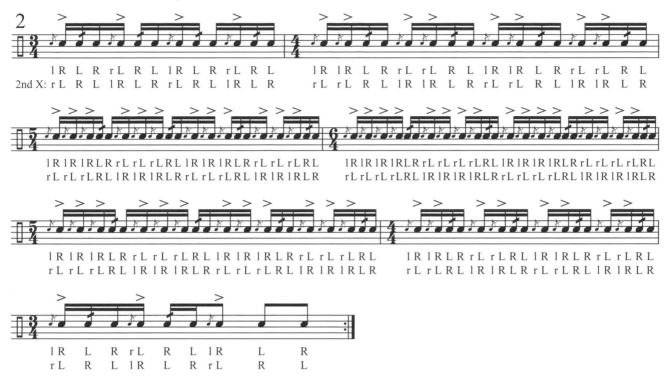

Here's the exercise with cheeses.

Here's the exercise with flam fives.

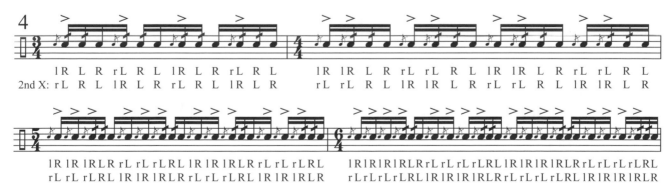

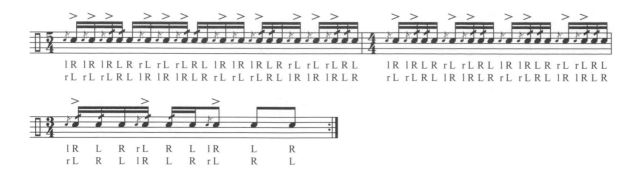

IR IR IRLR rL rL rLRL IR IR IRLR rL rL rLRL   IR IRLR rL rLRL IR IR IRLR rL rLRL
rL rL rLRL IR IR IRLR rL rL rLRL IR IR IRLR   rL rLRL IR IRLR rL rLRL IR IRLR

IR L R rL R L IR   L   R
rL R L IR L R rL   R   L

Consecutive Flams

Part 3: Inverted Motion

Now we're going to modify the consecutive flam exercise by removing one tap from the transitions. Instead of using a flam accent to shift from one hand to the next, we'll use an inverted flam tap.

The inverted flam tap requires the Moeller whipping motion in order to transition from a low tap to a high accent. This is normally done by the wrist with an upstroke, but at faster tempos there's too little time, so we'll need to replace the wrist motion with an arm motion in order to whip the stick in a hurry. It gets even trickier when we have multiple accents, where we'll need to whip into a series of free strokes. Using the new transitions, we'll cover the variations of the exercise, first with the accented flams spaced out and then with the accented flams adjacent.

The first variation (Exercise 1) has a tap between the accents. The biggest challenge is getting the stick up high to attack the first accent. Since the same hand plays a low tap immediately before the accent, there's very little time to lift the stick (at most tempos). This is where the Moeller whip stroke comes in to replace the wrist motion. In what I call the Moeller upstroke or "whip-prep" stroke, the forearm pumps up and down quickly in order to achieve the stick height necessary for the accent. It may feel a bit herky-jerky, but the upper arm and shoulders must engage to quickly throw the forearm up and immediately back down. The little bit of work done by the upper body is what allows the hand to stay completely relaxed as the stick gets whipped to the "up" position to play the next accent.

In most applications, the Moeller whip stroke is used for isolated accents in a "whip and stop" or "whip and flop" motion, but in these exercises it's more of a "whip and dribble" action. When there are two or more accents, it's crucial to whip into a free stroke that rebounds all the way back up to the same height for the next accent.

From there, be sure that the last accent is played as a concise downstroke. Try to stop the drumstick pointing toward the head, as that will be the key to initiating a stream of grace notes and/or taps at a low stick height. The low taps should be played as a smooth and even flow of 16th notes using plenty of finger control.

As with all of the exercises in these chapters, it's a good idea to separate the hands and isolate each section of the exercise. Put your practice pad on a couch cushion (or any quieter surface), and then play the accents to either side on the couch, with the low taps on the pad. When the exercise is played perfectly, you should hear a consistent stream of low 16th notes being played on the pad.

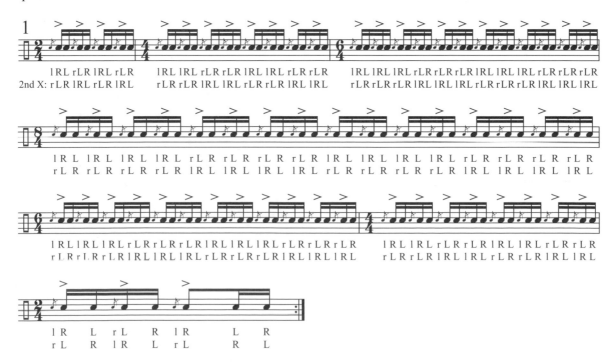

1

IRL rLR IRL rLR   IRL IRL rLR rLR IRL IRL rLR rLR   IRL IRL IRL rLR rLR rLR IRL IRL IRL rLR rLR rLR
2nd X: rLR IRL rLR IRL   rLR rLR IRL IRL rLR rLR IRL IRL   rLR rLR rLR IRL IRL IRL rLR rLR rLR IRL IRL IRL

IRL IRL IRL IRL rLR rLR rLR rLR IRL IRL IRL IRL rLR rLR rLR rLR
rLR rLR rLR rLR IRL IRL IRL IRL rLR rLR rLR rLR IRL IRL IRL IRL

IRL IRL IRL rLR rLR rLR IRL IRL IRL rLR rLR rLR   IRL IRL rLR rLR IRL IRL rLR rLR
rLR rLR rLR IRL IRL IRL rLR rLR rLR IRL IRL IRL   rLR rLR IRL IRL rLR rLR IRL IRL

IR L rL R IR   L   R
rL R IR L rL   R   L

A great variation for this exercise is to play a flammed diddle (also known as a cheese) on the accent. Be sure to accent both beats of the diddle and play them precisely—don't crush them.

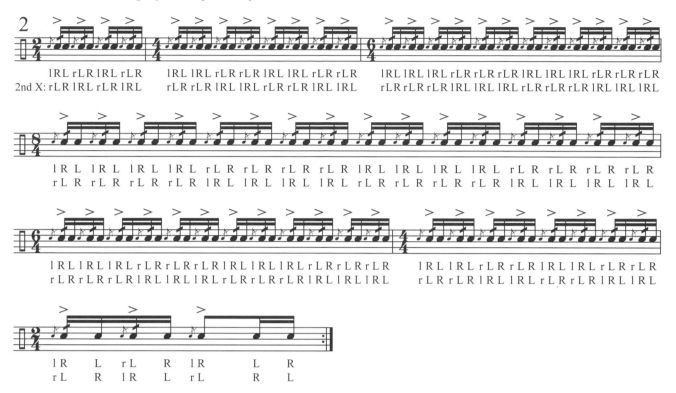

Now take out the taps between the flams so that they're adjacent. All of the rules from before apply, but there are new challenges in flam consistency and in maintaining the strength of the accents throughout the series of flams. Since the accents are strung together, some finger control will be necessary to aid the wrists so that the accents don't decrescendo.

If the first flam in a series is played accurately, generally the rest will follow suit. So it's key to coordinate the initial accent with the series of low taps. The last accent must be played with a downstroke for the maximum accent/tap differential. Be sure to use a metronome, tap your foot, and count quarter notes out loud throughout the exercises.

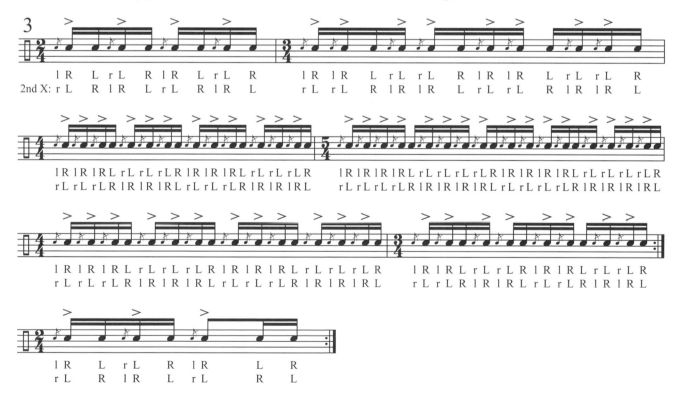

Finally, let's add the cheese for a fun variation.

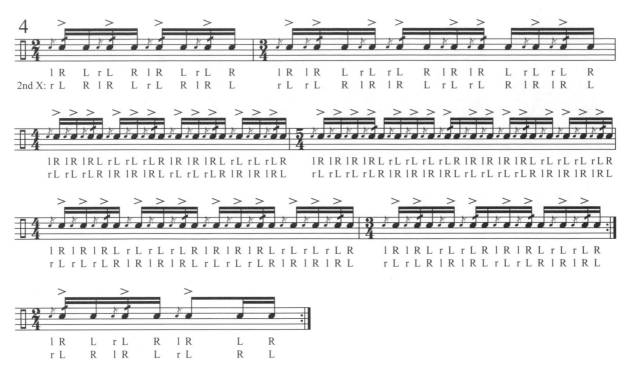

Consecutive Flams

Part 4: Hand-to-Hand Groupings

Next we're going to play hand-to-hand flams consecutively and in groups of two, three, and four. These exercises look simple on paper, and they are simple when played slowly. But when sped up they become challenging and test each hand's technique. To play the exercises quickly, each hand needs to negotiate accents and taps using Moeller whipping techniques. In addition to the main exercise, we've included some exercises for the individual hands.

Start these exercises slowly, using the four basic strokes: full (or free), down, tap, and up. Make sure that the stick heights are clearly separated between the accents and taps. The accents should return to about a vertical stick height, and the grace notes and taps should be played around 4" off the drum.

After mastering the exercises at slow tempos, take the tempo up and apply the modified Moeller techniques. You'll have to whip up into the first flam that each hand plays and then "no-chop flop-and-drop" out of the last flam that each hand plays. The faster you go, the more challenging it is to differentiate between the height and volume of accents and taps. But the more contrast you employ, the more musical you'll sound. Practice using the faster tempo's technique and make sure to use a metronome, tap your foot, and get comfortable counting quarter notes out loud.

Exercise 1 consists of four bars of 8th-note triplets. The sticking alternates at first, with sets of two, three, and four flams per hand. In the fourth bar, a group of four flams flips the sticking, and the exercise repeats with a left-hand lead.

At medium to fast tempos, the hand-to-hand flams in the first bar require the Moeller whip-and-flop technique. Whip the accents using the arm, and then smoothly flop down to the tap without impeding the stick's flow. Hold the sticks just tightly enough so as to not drop them, and use the arms to pump the quarter-note accents.

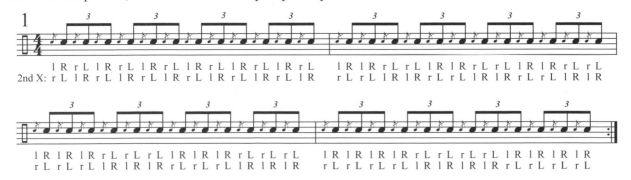

The next exercise isolates each hand and then combines them. Play it with a left-hand lead on the repeat. At medium to fast tempos, the sets of two, three, and four hand-to-hand flams in subsequent bars require what I call the Moeller "whip-to-free-stroke" technique. The arm whips the initial accent stroke, and the stick rebounds to a full stick height and comes back down with free strokes for equally powerful accents. Don't play the first accent harder than you can sustain on consecutive strokes. After the last accent in each grouping, flop down to the taps without impeding the stick's flow. The taps should be light and played as a smooth, even flow of triplets using finger control.

The last of the taps will be a Moeller upstroke. It may feel a bit herky-jerky, but the upper arm and shoulders must engage to quickly throw the forearm up and immediately back down. This little bit of work in the upper body allows the hand to stay completely relaxed as it gets whipped up for the next accent.

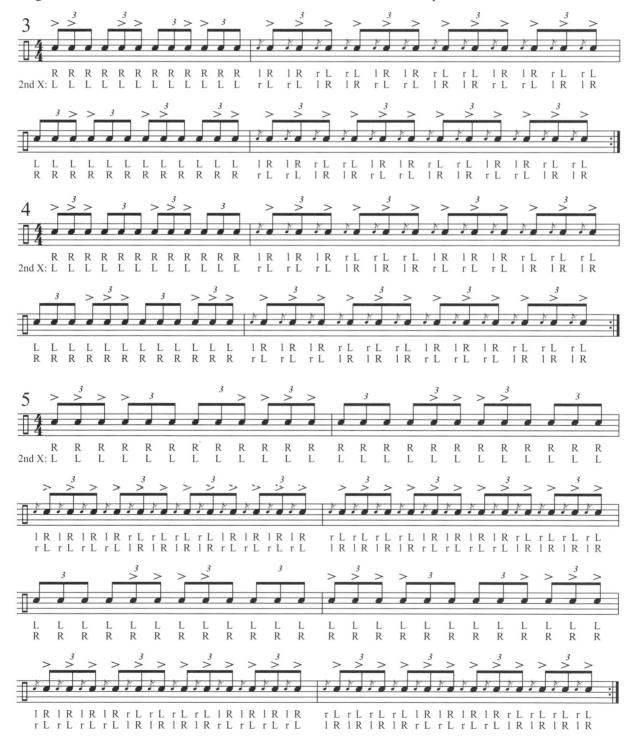

One-Sided Hairtas, Grandmas, and Grandpas

Three Hybrid Rudiments to Expand Vocabulary

Let's take a look at three unusual rudiments: one-sided hairtas, grandmas, and grandpas. These three closely related rudiments are especially useful for drumset fills when playing the accents on toms or cymbals and the unaccented notes on the snare. The unusual accent patterns can easily throw you off, so use a metronome, tap your foot, and count quarter notes out loud so that your pulse is grounded.

Here are the three rudiments.

One-Sided Hairta:

| R | L | R | | L | R | L | R | | L | R | L | R | | L | R | L | R | | L |
| L | R | L | | R | L | R | L | | R | L | R | L | | R | L | R | L | | R |

Grandma:

| R | L | R | R | L | R | L | R | R | L | R | L | R | R | L | R | L | R | R | L |
| L | R | L | L | R | L | R | L | L | R | L | R | L | L | R | L | R | L | L | R |

Grandpa:

| R | L | R | R | L | R | L | R | R | L | R | L | R | R | L | R | L | R | R | L |
| L | R | L | L | R | L | R | L | L | R | L | R | L | L | R | L | R | L | L | R |

One-sided hairtas are hairtas with the lead hand played as low taps while the secondary hand is accented. The resulting accent pattern is a syncopated rhythm that resembles a polyrhythm, however, each hand's role is simple. The lead hand plays low double beats using finger control while the secondary hand plays accented free strokes. The accents played by the secondary hand take up the space of an 8th note and should be played perfectly evenly. But focus more on the leading hand's rhythm in order to not lose track of the downbeats.

First we'll build the hairta, and then we'll add the accent pattern.

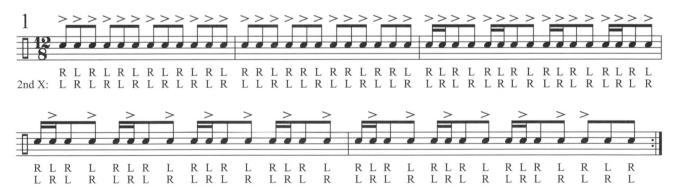

1

| R | L | R | L | R | L | R | L | R | L | R | L | | R | R | L | R | R | L | R | R | L | R | R | L | | R | L | R | L | R | L | R | L | R | L | R | L | R | L | R | L |
| 2nd X: L | R | L | R | L | R | L | R | L | R | L | R | | L | L | R | L | L | R | L | L | R | L | L | R | | L | R | L | R | L | R | L | R | L | R | L | R | L | R | L | R |

| R | L | R | | L | R | L | R | | L | R | L | R | | L | R | L | R | | L | | R | L | R | | L | R | L | R | | L | R | L | R | | L | R | L | R | | L |
| L | R | L | | R | L | R | L | | R | L | R | L | | R | L | R | L | | R | | L | R | L | | R | L | R | L | | R | L | R | L | | R | L | R | L | | L |

Next we'll look at the grandma. This rudiment consists of a paradiddle with an 8th-note release. The lead hand plays low taps, and the secondary hand plays accents. Again, focus on the rhythm of the lead hand, and try not to get thrown off by the evenly spaced accents played by the secondary hand.

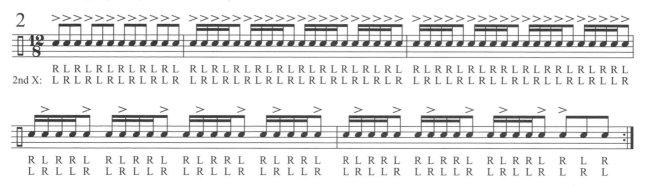

The grandpa is my answer to the grandma and has a slightly varied accent pattern that creates a shuffle. Both accents are played as downstrokes, and the fingers will be in charge of executing the inner beats.

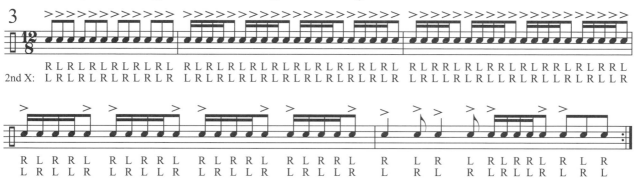

Now we'll combine all three rudiments into one exercise and switch to a duple feel using 8th notes and 16ths. Take this exercise slowly at first in order to fully understand the rhythms. Once comfortable, increase the speed and think of the pulse in half time.

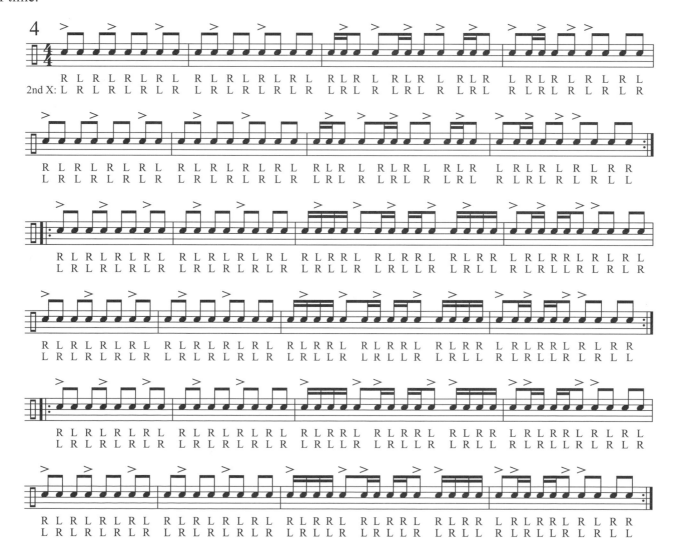

Nine Over Two

Part 1: Accenting the Quarter-Note Triplet

The simplest way to think about a nine-over-two polyrhythm is by dividing each partial of a quarter-note triplet into another triplet. In this chapter, we're adding accent patterns to this polyrhythm. Every accent, or group of accents, will fall within the underlying quarter-note triplet pulse. The goal is to become comfortable with the polyrhythm so that accent patterns sound smooth, natural, and musical.

Avoid blurring the transitions from one subdivision to the next, and play the patterns as precisely as possible with a metronome. The first example outlines the quarter-note triplet within each nine-note grouping.

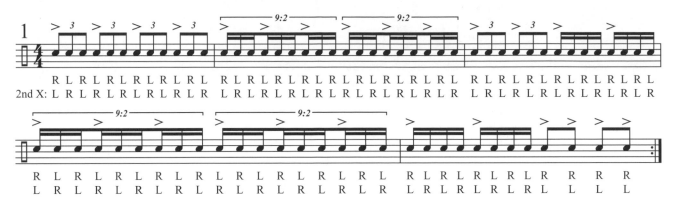

The next three variations accent one partial of each quarter-note triplet within the nine-note groupings.

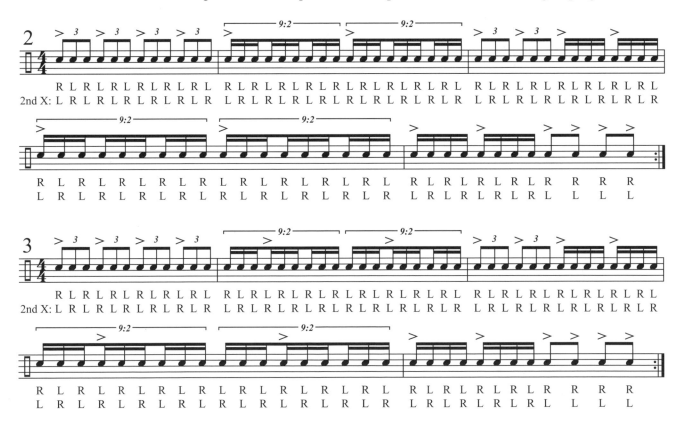

72

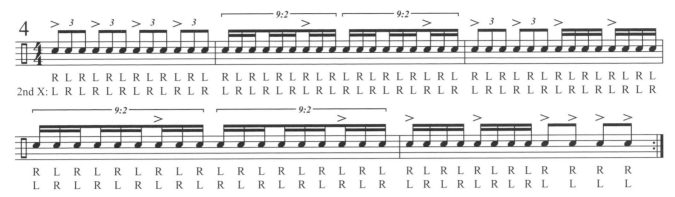

The next three variations accent two partials of each quarter-note triplet within the nine-note groupings.

Now we're going to accent all three partials of each quarter-note triplet within the nine-note groupings. In addition, we'll accent one entire triplet within each quarter-note triplet.

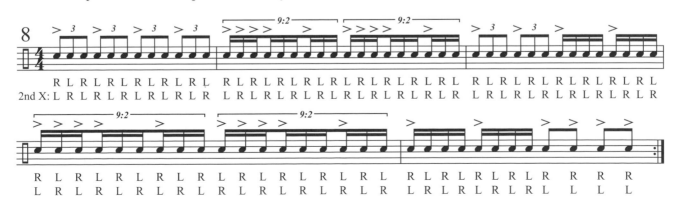

Finally, we'll accent two out of three triplets within the quarter-note triplet of each nine-note grouping.

Nine Over Two

Part 2: Sticking Variations

We're going to continue working with the nine-over-two polyrhythm by varying it with four different stickings: singles, "puh-duh-duhs" (RLL), triple strokes, and paradiddle-diddles. All of the exercises will incorporate an accent pattern leading into the nine-note grouping that outlines how the stickings are to be phrased within the polyrhythm.

We'll start with single strokes. It may help to put slight accents on the quarter-note triplets within the nine-note groupings at first so that you can keep track of where you are. However, you should ultimately strive for perfectly even free strokes.

```
         R L R L R L R L R L R L    R L R L R L R L R L R L    R L R L R L R L R L R L R L R L R L    R L R L R L R L R L R R
2nd X:   L R L R L R L R L R L R    L R L R L R L R L R L R    L R L R L R L R L R L R L R L R L R    L R L R L R L R L L
```

Next is the "puh-duh-duh" sticking (RLL). The leading hand should play evenly spaced free strokes across the bar, while the hand playing the low diddles should use a pumping forearm motion with finger control.

```
         R L R L R L R L R L R L    R L R L R L R L R L R L    R L L R L L R L L R L L R L L R L L    R L R L R L R L R L R R
2nd X:   L R L R L R L R L R L R    L R L R L R L R L R L R    L R R L R R L R R L R R L R R L R R    L R L R L R L R L L
```

The third sticking is triple strokes. Strive to make them sound perfectly even. You don't want three notes that bounce down in a decrescendo. Use quick finger control to add velocity to the second and third beats of each triple stroke.

```
         R L R L R L R L R L R L    R L R L R L R L R L R L    R R R L L L R R R L L L R R R L L L    R L R L R L R L R L R R
2nd X:   L R L R L R L R L R L R    L R L R L R L R L R L R    L L L R R R L L L R R R L L L R R R    L R L R L R L R L L
```

Our final sticking is the paradiddle-diddle. The accents within the nine-note grouping now fall on the half-note triplet. Use the accented half-note triplet pattern in the bar before the nines to feel your way through them. Focus on the initial accent of each paradiddle-diddle relative to the downbeats. If you know your paradiddle-diddles well, your muscle memory should take care of playing the inner beats evenly.

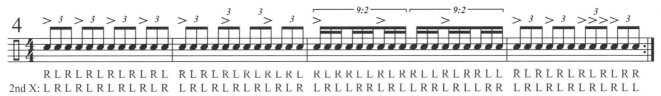

```
         R L R L R L R L R L R L    R L R L R L R L R L R L    R L R R L L R L R R L L R L R R L L    R L R L R L R L R L R R
2nd X:   L R L R L R L R L R L R    L R L R L R L R L R L R    L R L L R R L R L L R R L R L L R R    L R L R L R L R L L
```

Nine Over Two

Part 3: Incorporating the Half-Note Triplet

Now we're going to break up the polyrhythm by only playing six of the nine notes, using the half-note triplet as a framework. The figures, which are now six-note figures, will be isolated on each partial of the half-note triplet using each of our four sticking patterns from Part 2 of the previous chapter.

It's important to feel where the half-note-triplet accents fall relative to the downbeats. Exercise 1 will help you understand the rhythm's relationship to the pulse. First count the whole rhythm out loud while emphasizing the accents—"**1**-trip-let, 2-**trip**-let, 3-trip-**let**, 4-trip-let." Once this is comfortable, count quarter notes and half-note triplet accents—"1, 2-trip, 3-let,

4." Finally, count just the quarter notes while you play the half-note-triplet accent pattern. As always, use a metronome and tap your foot.

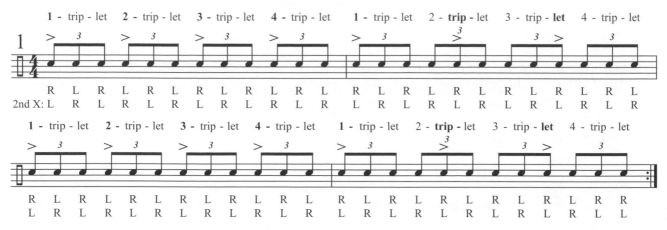

Now we're going to break up the polyrhythm by only playing six of the nine notes. We'll use each of the four nine-note stickings—singles, "puh-duh-duhs" (RLL), triple strokes, and paradiddle-diddles. Both the attack and release of each six-note grouping will always fall on a partial of the half-note triplet. Focus primarily on the accuracy of each of the six-note figures' first and last stroke, and make sure that the remaining notes always line up with the downbeat or half-note triplet partials.

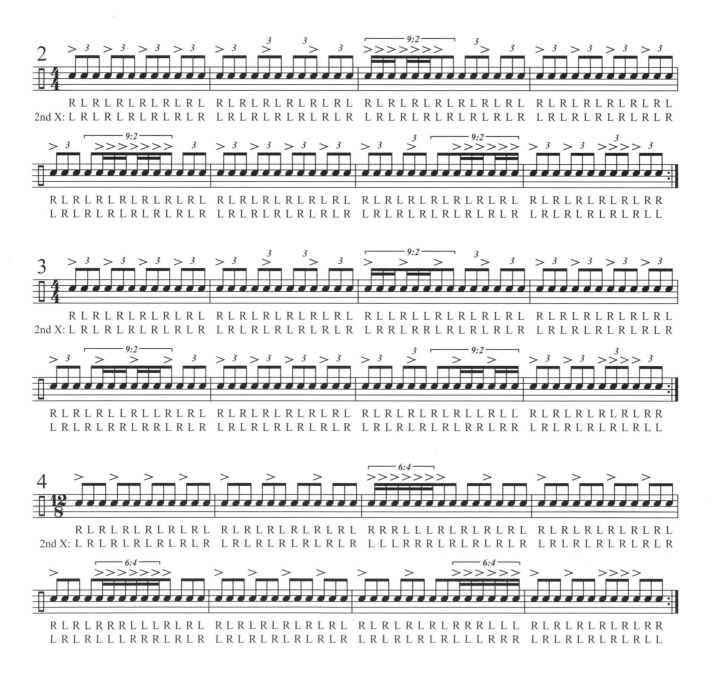

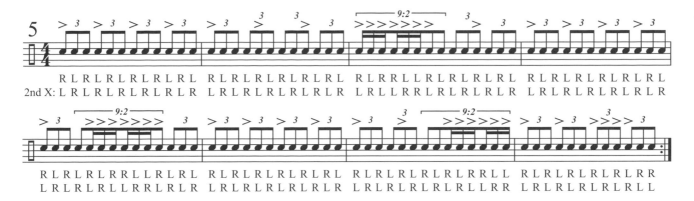

Finally, we're going to vary stickings within the nine-over-two polyrhythm in different combinations. Some use two different stickings, while others use three. There are many combinations, but for now we'll only look at a few. Afterward, come up with your own patterns. Remember to focus on the half-note or quarter-note triplet within each grouping.

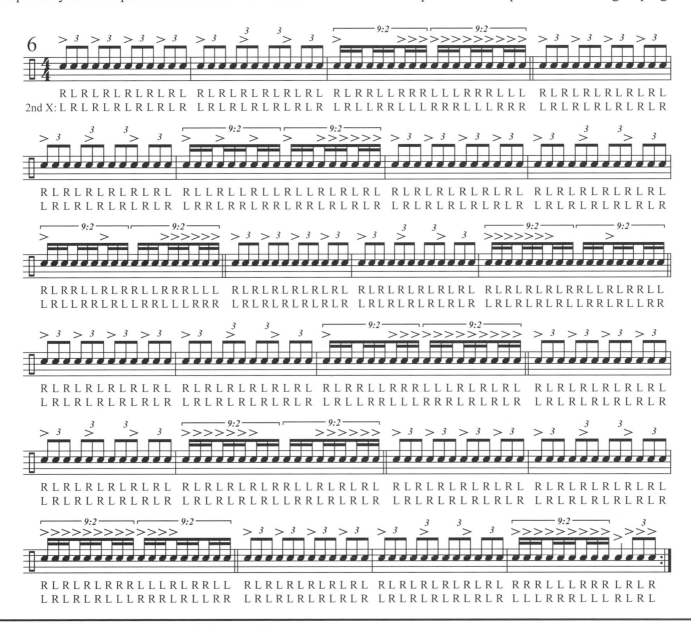

Flowing Into Diddles, Triple Strokes, and Paradiddles

Motions for Rudimental Transitions

These three exercises focus on transitioning into diddles, triple strokes, and paradiddles without changing the hand motion used to execute them. We'll use flowing free strokes borrowed from the eight-on-a-hand exercise to go into these rudiments, and we'll strive to maintain a relaxed rebounding stroke on the first note of the diddles and triple strokes and avoid slamming the downstroke on each paradiddle.

Let's start with diddles and triple strokes. I often see drummers attack diddles and triple strokes while applying additional pressure down into the drum. The idea is that if enough downward force goes into the first note then there will be energy left over for the second or third bounces. This is a good way to get started with these rudiments, but ultimately this approach will lead to weaker diddles and triple strokes that decrescendo, and they can also end up rhythmically crushed.

Here are some keys to playing high-quality, even, and balanced double and triple strokes.

1. Play the initial note as a pure free stroke without adding any extra force.

2. Let the first stroke rebound up as high as possible.

3. Use fingers to add velocity to the second stroke when playing triple strokes.

4. Finish with a powerful downstroke that points down into the drum. (Use the "alley-oop" technique for diddles and the "alley-oop-oop" technique for triple strokes.) At medium speeds and faster the first stroke will always be higher, but the greater velocity of the secondary strokes will enable them to match the volume of the first stroke.

At slower tempos it would make sense to use free strokes, but in these exercises we want to practice the faster tempo's technique slowly, so the last stroke should be played as a strict downstroke. I recommend using the American grip for better finger control so that you can play downstrokes by pulling the back end of the stick into the palm while holding the front end of the stick down with the thumb. Finally, don't squeeze too hard in the fulcrum. Try to feel the weight of the stick on the back fingers as the stick pivots under the thumb.

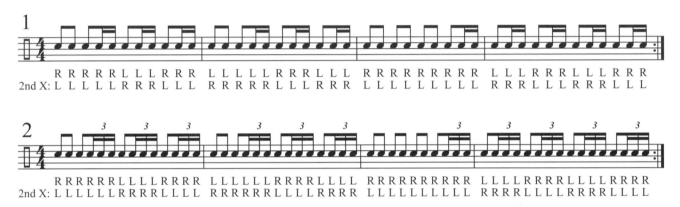

In this next variation, try to flow into each paradiddle's downstroke without changing the stroke type. A downstroke starts out exactly like a free stroke and should only become a downstroke after you hit the drum, so avoid adding the additional velocity, stick height, or inertia you might get from hitting harder. It's helpful to play downstrokes with the sticks pointing down toward the drum at about a 10-degree angle. This tilt adds some leverage and slightly reduces the rebound you have to contend with when stopping the stick low to the drum. Strive for consistent time and volume on each 8th-note count, and learn to count each of them out loud. When played accurately, it should sound like an eight-on-a-hand exercise with a few low 32nd notes tucked in between.

Velocity and Energy Shifters

8th-Note Paradiddle Transitions

We're going to combine flowing free-stroke 8th-note and paradiddle combinations using three different note rates. Along with the skills necessary to shift note rates accurately from one subdivision to the next, these exercises will also build the skills used to add or reduce energy in order to play perfectly in time. There is often a natural tendency for drummers to drag the tempo on harder or faster parts that require more energy or to rush less-busy parts that require little energy. Through practice and experience we learn to add energy to or subtract energy from different rhythms in order to play accurate time despite what may initially feel right or natural.

In the following exercises the 8th notes should be played as free strokes that rebound up as high as possible relative to the tempo. The attacks of the paradiddles should be the exact same stroke as the 8ths that preceded them, but immediately after hitting the drum they should be modified into strict downstrokes that point down toward the drumhead. Don't add any extra velocity or stiffness to this accent. All of the low diddles should be played lightly with fingers and use the "alley-oop" or "drop-catch" wrist-and-finger technique. As always, be sure to use a metronome in order to develop habits of accurate time, rhythm, and flow.

The first variation combines 8th notes and 16th-note paradiddles before finishing out the figures with diddles. The louder 8th notes require more energy than the low diddles, assuming that you're dribbling the rolls smoothly with fingers instead of a stiff stroke from the wrist. So be sure not to rush the less demanding low notes.

```
        R R R R L R R L L R R   L L L L L R L L R R L L   R R R R R R R   R L R R L L R R L L R R L L R R
2nd X:  L L L L L R L L R R L L   R R R R L R R L L R R   L L L L L L L L   L R L L R R L L R R L L R R L L
```

In this second variation we'll phrase the paradiddles into sextuplets. The energy required is similar between the 8th notes and sextuplets, so now it's a matter of knowing exactly how that rhythm sits as you transition into and out of it. If possible, try to feel a straight 8th-note subdivision when playing the sextuplet diddles. At this faster rate the downstroke will probably need to be played less strictly so that some of the accent's energy flows into the first diddle.

```
        R R R R L R R L L R R L L R R   L L L L L R L L R R L L R R L L   R R R R R R R   R L R R L L R R L L R R L L R R L L R R L L R R
2nd X:  L L L L L R L L R R L L R R L L   R R R R L R R L L R R L L R R   L L L L L L L L   L R L L R R L L R R L L R R L L R R L L R R L L
```

The final variation places the paradiddle into 32nd notes. Here the paradiddles and subsequent diddles require a good bit more energy than the 8th notes in order to not drag the tempo. The downstroke will need to be much less strict so that some energy can flow into the first diddle, so use more of what I call a "flop and drop" technique. Diddles at this speed will require a forearm-pumping motion to replace some of the wrist strokes so that there's no strain. Be sure to play the rolls lightly and low to the drum.

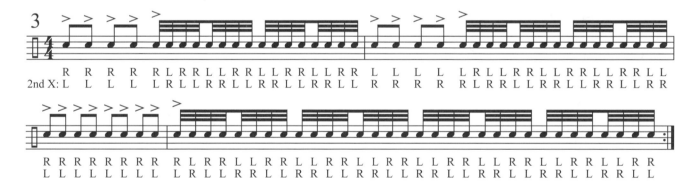

```
        R   R   R   R   R L R R L L R R L L R R L L R R   L   L   L   L   L R L L R R L L R R L L R R L L
2nd X:  L   L   L   L   L R L L R R L L R R L L R R L L   R   R   R   R   R L R R L L R R L L R R L L R R

        R R R R R R R   R L R R L L R R L L R R L L R R L L R R L L R R L L R R L L R R
        L L L L L L L   L R L L R R L L R R L L R R L L R R L L R R L L R R L L R R L L
```

Finally we'll play two exercises in which the paradiddle phrase's note rate changes each time so that you'll have to be ready to rhythmically switch gears and add or reduce energy on the fly to stay in time. Do your best to keep the motion of the accented notes big and high, and keep all of the taps and diddles low and light.

```
        R R R R L R R L L R R   L L L L L R L L R R L L R R L L   R R R R R R R   R L R R L L R R L L R R L L R R L L R R L L R R L L R R

        L L L L L R L L R R L L R R L L   R R R R L R R L L R R   L L L L L L L L   L R L L R R L L R R L L R R L L R R L L R R L L
```

Conclusion

Congratulations! You're now ready to go back to page 1 and do it all over again! Our human perceptions of rhythm and time are naturally flawed. While there's certainly beauty in the minor human imperfections, overall we really do need to continually brush up our interpretations of rhythm and time in order to make the music feel good and so that other musicians will want to play with us (especially in this digital age). As for the Chops Builders, these too are things that you can never play enough. Think of them as calisthenics that will keep your hands healthy for life (as long as they're played with a healthy technical approach as discussed in *Stick Technique*). Stagnant hands are sad hands, and nobody wants sad hands. So get on it!